Jennifer Serr

# C O M P L E T E

## Comprehension

### N O N F I C T I O N

# Teach

## Supporting Readers
## with Strategies

HEINEMANN
Portsmouth, NH

**Heinemann**

361 Hanover Street

Portsmouth, NH 03801–3912

www.heinemann.com

*Offices and agents throughout the world*

**A Note About Text Levels Assigned to Children's Books**

For the purposes of consistency, all children's books used for assessment in *Complete Comprehension: Nonfiction* were leveled through www.fountasandpinnellleveledbooks.com. Their leveling system is used by others across other leveling sites and apps, but the website is the only official source for F&P Text Level Gradient™ levels. If you use another leveling source, or rely on a different alphabetic leveling system without an official source, you may find discrepancies across different sites and apps.

Cataloging-in-Publication Data is on file at the Library of Congress.

ISBN: 978-0-325-10981-7

*Editors:* Zoë Ryder White and Heather Anderson

*Production:* Victoria Merecki

*Cover and interior designs:* Suzanne Heiser

*Cover art:* © Maxchered / Getty Images

*Photography:* Nicholas Christoff and Michelle Baker

*Videography:* Sherry Day, Michael Grover, and Dennis Doyle

*Typesetter:* Gina Poirier Design

*Manufacturing:* Steve Bernier and Val Cooper

Printed in the United States of America on acid-free paper

23  22  21  20  19  VP  1  2  3  4  5

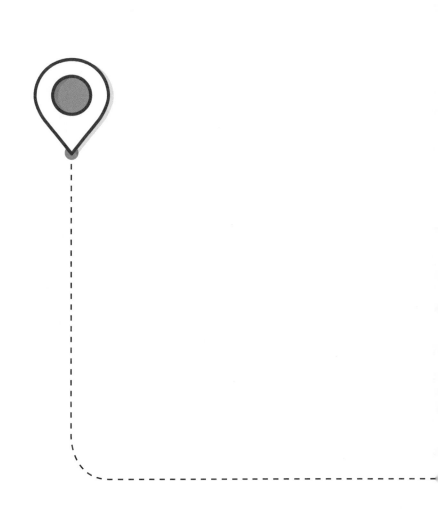

# Contents

# Strategies

## Main Idea 28

## Main Idea *continued*

To access the Online Resources, visit

**http://hein.pub/ccnonfic-login.**

Enter your email address and password (or click "Create New Account" to set up an account). Once you have logged in, enter keycode **WholeBooksNF** and click "Register."

# Text Features 114

# Text Features *continued*

# Introduction

**Y**ou have assessed. You have evaluated. Now you are ready to support readers in achieving the goals you have set with them. On the pages that immediately follow, you'll find:

**Teaching Toward Goals: 5 Steps:** a recommended sequence for planning and executing your instruction over time

**Q&A: Frequently Asked Questions About Teaching Toward Goals:** common questions about follow-up teaching

**Teaching Methods and Lesson Structures for Ongoing Instruction:** an overview of whole-class, small-group, and individual teaching options

After this introduction, you will find more than 100 strategies organized into five sections aligned to the goals listed in the box at the right.

If you have *The Reading Strategies Book* (Serravallo 2015), you will notice that the categories in this book match those in *The Reading Strategies Book*, so you could use relevant strategies from that book to support your goal-directed instruction as well. About twenty-five strategies that appear in that book also appear here because they are foundational. However, any similar strategies are explained in this book with new examples, charts, and lesson

 **Reading Engagement**

 **Main Idea**

 **Key Details**

 **Vocabulary**

 **Text Features**

language to offer you a unique way to teach. About seventy-five strategies in this book do not appear at all in *The Reading Strategies Book*.

## Teaching Toward Goals: 5 Steps

Once you determine a goal for a student, you are ready to gather ideas for strategies you may teach the student to help them reach that goal. Here are some concrete steps to follow:

1. **Gather Strategies.** Peruse the ideas beginning on page 19 of this book and choose ones that would be a "best fit" based on your goal for the student, the level of book the student is reading, and their level of proficiency with a skill. Record your choices on the And Now: Take It to the Conference section of the Planning Form shown below and available in the Online Resources.

2. **Confer in a Goal-Setting Conference.** Meet with the student, one-on-one, to discuss the results from the assessment and to decide together on a goal. In this meeting, you'll begin to support the student's goal by offering the first of what will be several strategies. Repeat

Planning Form (excerpt)

---

### And Now: Take It to the Conference

What goal or goals have you decided to focus on? (See Then column.)

*Vocabulary*

Which strategy or strategies will you introduce first? (Refer to pages from the Teaching Suggestions column.)

*V. 3 Lean on Text Features or V.5 Tricks for Spotting Clues in Context*

Additional notes to prepare (e.g., questions to ask, a book for modeling, and so on):

*Now you are ready to conduct a **Goal-Setting Conference** with this reader. Watch a video example of this type of conference at http://hein.pub/ccnonfic-login.*

---

this step with every reader you have assessed. For more information on the goal-setting conference, watch a video example available in the Online Resources.

3. **Plan Instruction Over Time.**
   Once you have students working on their individual goals, plan how you'll balance the ongoing whole-class, individual, and small-group teaching in the coming week(s). Find an overview of methods on pages 14–15, and watch a video example of each lesson type in the Online Resources. You can use the Planning Your Week

To access the Online Resources, visit

**http://hein.pub/ccnonfic-login.**

Enter your email address and password (or click "Create New Account" to set up an account). Once you have logged in, enter keycode **WholeBooksNF** and click "Register."

form shown on page 5, and available in the Online Resources, to get organized. For the lesson ideas you selected, choose a text or texts—quality literature—that you'll pull examples from or use for modeling. Often, you can reuse the text or texts for many lessons.

4. **Revisit, Reteach.** Don't expect the student to reach the goal you determined from the assessment in just one lesson. Whether you choose to teach the student in a whole-class, small-group, or individual setting—or some combination of those structures over time—chances are you will need to teach (and possibly reteach) multiple strategies to help the student reach the goal.

   After learning each strategy, the student will have a chance to practice and apply it in multiple contexts. Over time, you'll likely decrease the amount of support you provide, and the student will increase their independence. Let a couple of days pass before revisiting a lesson, so that the student has the opportunity to use the strategy, approximate, and adjust. Reteach strategies if a student needs support, and move on to a new strategy for the same goal when they are ready. Your aim should be to help students build a repertoire of ways to work toward their goals.

**5. Reassess.** This is where the assess-evaluate-teach loop comes full circle. Once you've taken steps 1 to 4, you will be able to see when a student has shown proficiency and independence with the goal(s) and may be ready to move on to more challenging books. For more guidance, see *Assess*, pages 16–19.

### Planning Your Week

| | Monday | Tuesday | Wednesday | Thursday | Friday |
|---|---|---|---|---|---|
| **Minilesson** (every day— 10 minutes) | MI. 2 – what/ So what | MI. 4 Heading | Repertoire repeat 2, 4. | MI. 9 Text Feature Addition | MI. 15 Scan TOC |
| **Strategy Lesson** (10 minutes) | Drucella Kamil Jason Joseph V. 3 ⑩ | | Dorian Anthony Shayna KD. 18 ⑩ | TBD | Dean Janelle T. 12 ⑩ |
| **Strategy Lesson** (10 minutes) | | Homayrist Sammie ⑩ | TBD | Homayrist Sammie ⑩ | TBD |
| **Conferences** (5 minutes each) | Destiny Ezekiel Wilson ⑮ | Kamil Jason Hazel Dean ⑮ | Justin Elijah Drucella Joseph ⑳ | Nayeli Anthony Richard Wilson ⑳ | |
| **Guided Reading** (15–20 minutes) | | | | | |
| **Other** (10 minutes) Partnership | Elijah + Semaj ⑤ Daisy + Ingrid ⑤ | Pharoah + Jose ⑤ Justin + Richard ⑤ | | Nayeli + Hazel ⑤ Angel + Jeremiah ⑤ | |
| **Read-Aloud** (every day— 20 minutes) | What's Eating You? (Davies) pp 1–8 | pp 9–15 | pp 16–19 | re-read + whole-class conversation | pp 20–25 |

40 minutes

May be photocopied for classroom use. Copyright © 2019 by Jennifer Serravallo from *Complete Comprehension: Nonfiction*. Portsmouth, NH: Heinemann.

Planning Your Week Form

## Q&A: Frequently Asked Questions About Teaching Toward Goals

I collected the following questions from teachers who have used this resource. I highly recommend you skim them now and then return to them if questions of your own arise. Some of my answers cover actions you might want to consider before you start teaching.

**Q.** *How can I plan for teaching over time?*

**A.** Once your students know their goals, you'll be ready to plan for ongoing instruction. My first recommendation is to try to see your class at a glance, using a simple form, like the Class Profile on page 7, and available in the Online Resources. On this form, record your class list, the text level or level range each student is able to read, and the primary goal you want to work toward with each student. This enables you to identify students with common goals. You can also think through whole-class lesson ideas and small-group lesson ideas and then record them at the bottom of the form.

**Grouping Readers** In general, when I group students, I am less concerned about them all reading books at the same level than I am about whether the strategies I choose are applicable to all of them. On pages 19–144, you'll find more than 100 lesson ideas, most of which are appropriate for students reading books of any level. Those strategies that are best for a particular level range (e.g., J–M or N–R) are indicated as such.

> Even if you have not yet assessed every student, get started right away with your teaching plans.

## Class Profile

| Whole-Class Lesson Ideas |
| --- |
| Focus for the week - Determining Main Idea |
| MI.2 - What / So what |
| MI.4 - Understand Clever Headings |
| MI.9 - Text Feature Addition |
| MI.15 - Scan Table of Contents |
| |
| |
| |

### Small Group

| Names | Lesson Ideas |
| --- | --- |
| Drucella, Kamil, Jason, Joseph | vocab—<br>V.3 Lean on Text features |
| | |
| Dorian, Anthony, Shayna | compare contrast<br>K.D. 18 - Venn Diagram |
| | |
| Dean, Janelle | text features - connect to text<br>T.12 visualize Maps by<br>connecting to text |
| | |
| | |
| | |

May be photocopied for classroom use. Copyright © 2019 by Jennifer Serravallo from *Complete Comprehension: Nonfiction*. Portsmouth, NH: Heinemann.

## Class Profile

| Name | | Level | Goal and Notes |
| --- | --- | --- | --- |
| Pharoah | ✓ | R | vocab - in complex sentences |
| Joe | ✓ | R? | * assess |
| Sammie | ✓✓ | P | engagement |
| Elijah | ✓✓ | L | vocab - context |
| Richard | ✓✓ | M | MI - part |
| Drucella | ✓✓ | N/O | vocab - use TF |
| Angel | ✓ | S/T | |
| Jeremiah | ✓ | T | * assess |
| Destiny | ✓ | Q | * assess |
| Kamil | ✓✓ | M | vocab - use TF |
| Ezekiel | ✓ | R | MI - whole book synthesis |
| Justin | ✓✓ | M | |
| Daisy | | P? | |
| Jason | ✓✓ | L/M | MI - part / vocab |
| Nayeli | ✓✓ | K | MI - whole |
| Dorian | ✓ | M | KD - compare/contrast |
| Wilson | ✓✓ | M | Key Details |
| Homayris | ✓✓ | N | engagement |
| Jason | ✓ | O | vocab - using features |
| Joseph | ✓✓ | M | vocab / TF |
| Hazel | ✓✓ | K | MI + KD |
| Dean | ✓✓ | K | text features - study photos |
| Anthony | ✓✓ | L | KD - compare/contrast |
| Ingrid | ✓ | P | KD - supporting MI |
| Shayna | ✓ | M/N | KD - compare + contrast |
| Janelle | ✓ | M | TF - synthesize w/ main text |
| Semaj | ✓ | L/M | MI - supporting / proving |
| | | | |
| | | | |

May be photocopied for classroom use. Copyright © 2019 by Jennifer Serravallo from *Complete Comprehension: Nonfiction*. Portsmouth, NH: Heinemann.

> When grouping students, be mindful of their goals and the levels of the texts they are choosing to read. The rubrics in *Evaluate* and recommended level ranges indicated in the margins next to each strategy in this book will help you to make good lesson choices.

> Notice that the students in this text features group are reading books at Levels K–M. They were grouped in part because the demands on readers in texts at these levels are similar.

**Planning Your Week**  Now it is time for the detailed planning of your week. I plan on a daily whole-class interactive read-aloud and minilesson. The read-aloud typically lasts about twenty minutes, and I use a small number of strategies during that time. The minilesson typically lasts about ten minutes, during which time I focus on just one specific strategy that would benefit most of my students. You might choose small-group lesson topics based on student goals, as a result of

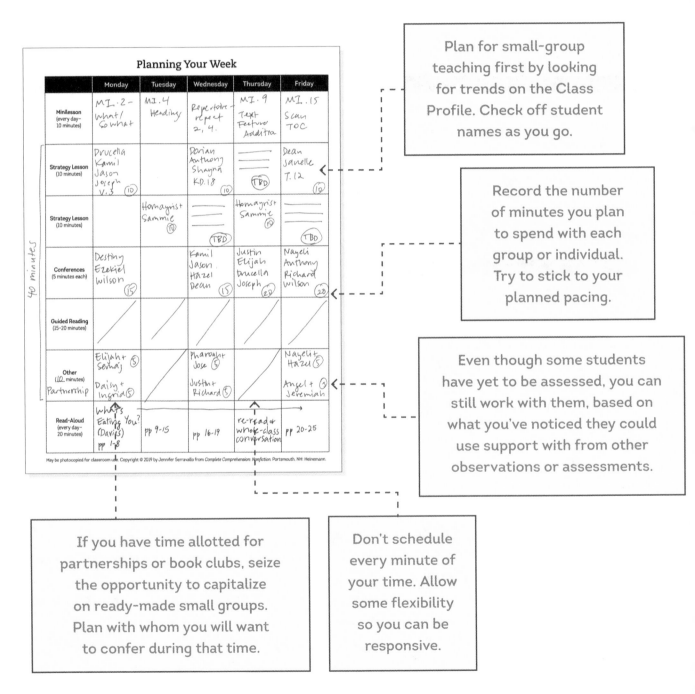

Plan for small-group teaching first by looking for trends on the Class Profile. Check off student names as you go.

Record the number of minutes you plan to spend with each group or individual. Try to stick to your planned pacing.

Even though some students have yet to be assessed, you can still work with them, based on what you've noticed they could use support with from other observations or assessments.

If you have time allotted for partnerships or book clubs, seize the opportunity to capitalize on ready-made small groups. Plan with whom you will want to confer during that time.

Don't schedule every minute of your time. Allow some flexibility so you can be responsive.

*Complete Comprehension* or other assessments, or possibly use that time
to support goals from your reading curriculum.

Strategy lessons, conferences, and guided reading are the places
where I differentiate instruction. How many of these structures I
use each day will vary based on the needs of my class. For example, if
many of my students have common goals, then I'll support them with
those during the whole-class minilessons. If most of my students'
goals are unique, and the range of levels of books they are reading is
wide, then I'll probably do lots of conferring. Also, each week might
look a little bit different, again, based on the needs of my class. One
week I may find myself doing many strategy lessons, and the next
week mostly one-on-one conferences.

As a rule of thumb, I try to see every student in an individual
conference at least *twice a month* and to see every student either in a
small group or individual conference at least *twice a week*.

I enter students' names in the Planning Your Week form (page 8), starting with those who have common goals and are reading similar levels of text, and organize them for small-group lessons. Then I add the names of students for partnership and book-club conferences. Finally, I record who I plan to see in individual conferences. I keep an eye on how much time I've allotted for all of my conferences and small groups. If you'd like to read more about the teaching structures mentioned here, see pages 14–15. You can view video examples of each structure in the Online Resources.

## Q. *How do I choose model texts for teaching?*

A. Any article or nonfiction book can work as a model text in your lessons. A good rule of thumb, however, is to choose one that is familiar to you and your students. That way, students will be able to focus on the lesson topic rather than on figuring out the

content of the book. Short texts, such as articles, are great to use as models, since they allow you to zoom in on a bit of text that elucidates your teaching point. However, do not use books that are part of this kit, because they may be used later by some students during assessment, and studying the text as a class may give you a false read on how much a student is able to understand independently, without instructional support.

You may notice that occasionally the model text that I have selected to use in the How I'd Teach It section of each strategy page is outside the range of levels suggested for the strategy. That is because the text I read to students and use in lesson examples needn't always be the same level as the texts students are choosing to read. It is possible to do deeper thinking in a lower-level text, and sometimes, choosing shorter texts for demonstration saves time in the lesson and helps children return to their independent reading more quickly.

**Q.** *While I'm working with students in small groups and conferences, what is the rest of the class doing?*

**A.** I'm convinced that reading is the best activity for students to be engaged in while you're doing your differentiated instruction. Not centers, not worksheets, not writing responses—reading! Ideally, that reading is of their own choosing and is a text they can read with accuracy, fluency, and comprehension. This will help in more ways than one:

- First, it allows students time to practice the strategies you've taught them, which will help them reach their individual goals.

- It allows students to work on their stamina and read a high volume of texts. Voluminous reading supports growth.

- It frees you up to immerse yourself fully in the work of supporting individuals and groups. In a typical reading block of thirty-five to forty minutes, I try to support about ten readers. I can't be that focused or productive if I'm trying to manage what the other readers in the class are doing; they need to be taught to read and work independently toward their goals.

## Q. *What's the best way to keep track of my assessments and teaching over time?*

A. I recommend that you establish a note-taking and record-keeping system—one that makes sense to you and that you are able to use and maintain easily. I like to be able to see each child's learning over time at a glance. So I keep a separate folder for each student, in which I store all my individual assessments, along with anecdotal records I write during conferences and small-group lessons.

Other teachers find it helpful to create a notebook or section in a binder for each student, or store notes in a bin or file. When it comes time to meet with a particular student for a conference or in a small group, you can simply pull the notebook/folder/binder from its storage space and bring it to wherever the teaching is happening. Keeping notes this way also allows you to share them with other teachers who work with your students (e.g., English as a second language teachers, resource room teachers, intervention specialists).

Some teachers prefer taking notes online or with apps such as Google Drive, Pensieve, Confer, or Evernote. If utilizing an online note-taking system, it will be important to find one that has cloud-based storage to allow any teacher who is working with a student to access shared notes.

## Q. *I know what my student needs. How and where do I begin?*

A. Setting clear goals has been shown by many researchers to be one of the most influential things you can do as a teacher (Petty 2006; Wiggins and McTighe 2001; Pink 2009). Goals are motivating, help us maintain clear focus, establish the conditions for faster progress, and allow for instant accountability of ourselves and our students. For that reason, the goal-setting conference is key; during this meeting, I lead students to reflect on their written responses about reading, support them in choosing a goal, and get each student started with a new goal. I hope you'll confer with each student before moving ahead with ongoing teaching. Learn more about the goal-setting conference by watching a video example in the Online Resources.

## Teaching Methods and Lesson Structures for Ongoing Instruction

As you select strategies for supporting students' goals, consider options from this section, which includes the teaching structures I rely on most for whole class, small groups, and individuals.

Any of the strategies in the five goal sections that begin on page 16 can be taught using any of the lesson structures described on pages 14–15. (Watch a video example of each type of lesson in the Online Resources, or read more in *Understanding Texts & Readers*, pages 233–246 [Serravallo 2018].)

Your choice of structure will be based on how many students need to work on the strategy you've chosen and how much support each child needs. If many or most of your students need support, you would likely choose from among the whole-class structures. If only a few need it, you would likely select a small-group structure. Think of it this way: choose your methods to match your purpose.

Keep in mind, also, that the texts recommended on each strategy page are just that: recommendations. You by no means need to use those texts. Feel free to choose what I suggest or to choose your own—and use texts across lesson ideas as frequently as you like.

# Lesson Structures

## INTERACTIVE READ-ALOUDS

**Group size:** Small group or whole class

*Especially good for:*

- Showing students how to orchestrate many strategies
- Providing a lot of support for a new goal
- Providing opportunities for readers to deepen comprehension through conversation
- Supporting thoughtful annotating and note-taking

**See the Online Resources for a video demonstration.**

## VIDEO-ALOUDS

**Group size:** Small group or whole class

*Especially good for:*

- Engaging students in reading a nontraditional "text"
- Introducing new strategies
- Providing a lot of support for a new goal

**See the Online Resources for a video demonstration.**

## MINILESSONS

**Group size:** Whole class

*Especially good for:*

- Introducing a strategy and inviting students to try it
- Reteaching a strategy that is challenging students

**See the Online Resources for a video demonstration.**

## GUIDED READING

Group size: Small group of three to four students

*Especially good for:*

- Giving a group of students experience with a text that's more challenging than what they read now
- Supporting students who are emergent bilinguals
- Supporting students with a new genre or text type

**See the Online Resources for a video demonstration.**

## PARTNERSHIP AND BOOK-CLUB CONFERENCES

**Group size:** Small group of two to four students

*Especially good for:*

- Holding students accountable for ongoing work around their goals
- Helping students and their peers share and work collaboratively toward goals
- Supporting students with conversation skills alongside their comprehension goal(s)

**See the Online Resources for a video demonstration.**

## SMALL-GROUP STRATEGY LESSONS

**Group size:** Small group of two to three students

*Especially good for:*

- Providing guided practice for students so they can transfer skills to independent reading
- Teaching students who have a common goal
- Holding students accountable for ongoing work around their goals

**See the Online Resources for a video demonstration.**

## CLOSE READING

**Group size:** Small group or whole class

*Especially good for:*

- Introducing a challenging text in a supportive forum in which students can learn comprehension strategies they can use when they read independently
- Supporting thoughtful annotating and note-taking
- Encouraging careful rereading

**See the Online Resources for a video demonstration.**

## INDIVIDUAL CONFERENCES

**Group size:** One student

*Especially good for:*

- Checking in with an individual student to monitor progress with a strategy, skill, and/or goal
- Holding a student accountable for ongoing work around their goal
- Reteaching strategies or offering new strategies that support the goal

**See the Online Resources for a video demonstration.**

# Reading Engagement

Research supports what we know in our hearts to be true: Our reading lessons might be wonderful, but unless they help students apply what we've taught and guide them to become independent, our lessons really haven't helped students much. (See, for example: Guthrie and Wigfield 1997; Ford 1992; Flippo 2001; Allington 2012.)

The assessment you just finished evaluating helped you to learn about your students' comprehension. And sometimes, when a student struggles to understand a book, it reveals itself in their engagement—or lack thereof. (It's boring not to understand, after all!) Sometimes, engagement in and of itself will pose a challenge.

The reflection questions students answered at the end of the assessment may also help you learn about whether a student needs support with engagement. Recall that students were asked to reflect about whether the book was a good fit, whether they liked it, and whether they'd choose another book like it from the library. If a student has a hard time articulating responses, that student may need support finding other books that would increase their engagement.

## Book Choice

Most adults can remember times when finishing a book took much longer than it should have. The book may have sat on your night-stand as you slowly chipped away at it, or maybe you tucked the book on a shelf and never finished it. We need to help support readers in our class with their book choices so that they find ones they'll love, ones that are both enjoyable and readable, so that they support comprehension and hold the reader's attention.

## Focus

The classroom can be filled with distractions—announcements; unexpected visitors at the door; other students moving around, get-ting things from their desks, coughing. And when our students go home to read, there will be little sisters and grown-ups asking them questions and electronics calling their names. For a successful read-ing life, students need to be able to block out potential distractions and maintain concentration in their book, notice if and when they do get distracted, and have ways to reengage.

## Monitoring for Meaning

Engagement in reading is inextricably linked to comprehension. When a reader is engaged, they are making a movie in their minds, imagining the information the author is teaching about. Children need to learn to notice when their comprehension falters and must have ways to fix it.

## Stamina

Readers get better at reading by reading! Although we may set aside long stretches of time for children to read each day, some students will need to build up to the amount of time we set aside and may need strategies for reading the whole time.

# Strategies for Reading Engagement at a Glance

# Reflect on Your Reading Identity

**Strategy** To get ready to choose new books, reflect on who you are as a reader. Think: "What do I like? What do I dislike? When has reading been awesome? When has reading not been awesome?" Jot: "I'm the kind of reader who . . . When I read, I usually choose . . . Books that used to work for me were . . . but now. . . ."

**What it is** Too often, students self-identify as a level, rather than understanding that levels are for books, not readers. If you catch a child referring to themselves as a level, or you notice they could use support articulating aspects of their reading identity, you have the power to change this.

**How I'd teach it** After modeling your own reflections about yourself as a reader, have students try. Perhaps they have a reading log to look back on to notice what books they've finished and which they've abandoned, or maybe you've asked them to complete a reading interest inventory. Ask students to reflect on themselves as readers by doing some quick jotting in their notebooks using this strategy. If it would help, consider presenting them with sentence starters such as, "I'm the kind of reader who . . ." or "When I read, I find that I choose . . ." or "The books that have worked best for me in the past are . . . and/but now I'm finding. . . ." After jotting their reflections, they can use them to help with book selections.

From *Understanding Texts & Readers* (Serravallo 2018)

Who is this for?

LEVELS
J–W

SKILL
book choice

# E.2

# Use Book Talks to Help Book Choices

**LEVELS**

J–W

**SKILL**

book choice

**Strategy** As you choose books and as you talk about books with your friends, think about what you've heard about the book from others. Consider whether or not you connect to characters, a theme, or something else you've heard about the book.

**What it is** Seymour Simon, Nicola Davies, Nic Bishop, Melissa Stewart—there's a reason these authors are so well known by children. Every book they write is so engaging and they get passed along from reader to reader with excitement. But sometimes, if we look closely at our classroom library's nonfiction section, we find books collecting dust. Is that because those books are uninteresting, or is it just because they have not yet been made popular? When you want to highlight some books in your library, do book talks to get kids excited about them.

**How I'd teach it** You might do the book talks yourself at first, and then invite students to assume the role. Teach them persuasive language that would convince others to pick up the book. Then, as students approach the classroom library or school library to make their book selections, they can remember what they heard about books from you or their peers, and use the book talks to help them make their choices.

Book talks can be done as a whole class, or in small groups, grouping kids based on what you know to be the range of texts they tend to be able to read with confidence. After talking the books up, display them prominently on the chalkboard ledge or on top of a bookshelf and watch them disappear!

# Pre-Plan Stop-and-Think Spots

E.3

**Strategy** Think about your reading goal. Put some sticky notes throughout your book. When you get to each note, you might stop and think, jot, or sketch connected to your goal.

**What it is** Putting sticky notes at several spots throughout a book reminds students they should be stopping to monitor for meaning. Seeing a note encourages readers to refocus their attention if it has wavered. Notes can serve as simple reminders to stop and think or as cues to do some jotting connected to the comprehension goal. They can also be used as cues to draw a quick sketch or symbol (e.g., a smiley face for a part students liked, an exclamation point for a spot that surprised them); these same notes can then be used as conversation starters in partnerships or book clubs, or as entry points for students to discuss their reading work with you during conferences or small-group instruction.

## How I'd teach it

During a conference, and then independently, have students fill their books with about ten blank sticky notes that will serve as reminders for them to stop, check their understanding, and resume reading. Notes can remain blank, or you can jot short, open-ended prompts on them that align with the goal. For example, a child with a text features goal might jot, "Connect photo to text?" or simply "Feature?"

Barbara Golub

*Who is this for?*

LEVELS
J–W

SKILLS
focus,
monitoring for
meaning

# E.4

# Catch Your Running Mind

## Who is this for?

### LEVELS

J–W

### SKILLS

focus,
monitoring for
meaning

**Strategy**  When you notice your mind wandering as you read, pause. Go back to the last place you remember reading with understanding and reread from there.

**What it is**  For some students, distractibility and lack of focus are impediments to engaged reading. Giving them explicit instruction on how to monitor their own attention, and helping them feel successful with short-term goals, can improve their stamina and focus.

**How I'd teach it**  This is a difficult strategy to demonstrate because you can't show students your mind wandering as you read. Instead, saying the strategy in clear steps, and describing what it feels like when your mind is wandering, can help students know when to apply the strategy.

**Tip**  Some students have a difficult time realizing when their mind is wandering or when they are getting distracted. It may help to keep these students near you during one reading period. Give them a silent "eyes-back-in-your-book" reminder when you notice distraction. Your frequent and consistent feedback will help students start to catch themselves when attention wavers.

Merridy Gnagey

# Read, Pause, Retell

**Strategy**   Place a sticky note ahead in your book. Read up to it, and pause. Retell to yourself what you just read and/or give yourself a stretch break. Move the sticky note ahead and repeat.

**What it is**   Few readers are going to be able to automatically sit down and sustain forty minutes of reading time if they aren't accustomed to it. For those students who lose steam, get sleepy, or fade in and out while reading, there is a way of teaching them to pace themselves. Setting breaks along the way, with a very short task to monitor or work on comprehension when they take a break, can support their ability to focus. As they continue with the strategy, it'll be important to increase the number of pages or amount of time in between the breaks over time.

**How I'd teach it**   Say to students: "We can place a sticky note just a few pages ahead. Then we can keep our eyes in the book until we get to that note. We can retell to ourselves, or take a short movement break (quick stretch, look around, stand and sit), then set a new page to read up to by moving the blank sticky note."

You can ask students to reflect upon how many pages they typically read before needing a break—perhaps suggesting they look at a reading log if they keep one—and have them start there. Without judgment, celebrate whatever they say: "One page? Two? Great! Put a sticky note after that number of pages." Then check in a few days later and decide together if the breaks can become less frequent.

*Lauren Knoke*

**Who is this for?**

LEVELS
J–W

SKILLS

focus,
monitoring
for meaning,
stamina

## E.6 The Look and Feel of Independent Reading Time

**LEVELS**

J–W

**SKILLS**

focus, stamina

**Strategy** Pay attention to what your independent reading looks and feels like. Notice if your eyes and mind are on the book, and if not, refocus yourself.

**What it is** It's important to set students up with clear expectations for their independent reading time. Often, teachers decide to have class discussions about what independent reading time looks and sounds like, what students should do if they are having trouble, and how students could fix their trouble independently and get back to reading. If you notice many students aren't making the best use of their reading time, this might be a whole-class lesson. If it's just a few students who need this support, consider pulling them into a small group.

**How I'd teach it** I'd admit to kids that all readers, including me, sometimes hit slumps, and that there are endless pulls on our attention these days. The important thing to remember for a successful independent reading time is that we are in charge of our own minds—we have to monitor our concentration, notice if it's fading, and get back to reading. Decide as a class (or a small group) the things you consider to be independent reading "non-negotiables," and chart the expectations for reading time.

**Tip** Not all engaged reading looks the same. For some students, allowing them the chance to wiggle, fidget, stand, bounce on balls, or engage in some other gross motor activity while reading could support their attention and focus.

Merridy Gnagey

# Set a Timer

**Strategy** Think about how long you can read before giving yourself a break. Set a timer. Read until time's up. Take the break you need. Set the timer again, perhaps for slightly longer this time!

**What it is** Personal timers can help us set short-term goals that are time based, not page based. Give students working on their reading stamina their own personal timers. (My favorites are the silent Time Timers—small timers that don't make a sound when time is up and don't require the child to know how to tell time.)

**How I'd teach it** I'd acknowledge that the reading block is long—and that sometimes it's hard to get a sense of how long we've been reading, and how much longer there is to go; therefore, it's not always easy to know how much energy and attention we'll need to devote to the task. A timer can give us a visual check as we're developing an internal sense of time.

**Tip** Some readers will just need the visual of a timer set for the entire time, with either minutes ticking down or a red screen shrinking (in the case of the Time Timer). Other readers can benefit from using the timer to set shorter part-of-the-reading-time goals. For example, if the entire reading period is forty minutes, perhaps they set the timer for every ten, and after those ten minutes they could take some sort of physical break (e.g., a walk around the classroom, a trip to get a drink of water, a short stretch at their table).

Kelly Boyle

## Who is this for?

**LEVELS**

J–W

**SKILLS**

focus, stamina

# E.8

# Losing Reading Steam?
# Read a "Break" Text

## Who is this for?

**LEVELS**

J–W

**SKILLS**

focus, stamina

**Strategy**  If you notice your attention shifting, or your energy fading, swap the longer book you're reading for something short. Read from your "break" text (magazine, poem, fiction, etc.) for a few minutes. When you feel ready, refocus and jump back into your chapter book.

**What it is**  A core principle of this assessment and teaching resource is that longer works require a reader to do more synthesis, more accumulation of text, and more carrying forward of information. For students who are still warming up to the stamina for longer works, you can vary the materials they read, keeping students reading the whole time.

**How I'd teach it**  Tell students to keep a magazine, poem, short story, newspaper, or some other short text with them. Describe what it feels like to be losing energy for reading, or getting out of the focused state. Offer them the option to swap reading materials to keep their reading going.

**Tip**  Keep an eye on readers who are switching between reading materials, and make sure that it doesn't negatively impact their overall ability to comprehend; pay special attention to their comprehension of the longer book. For some readers, the "break" text is best if it's in a different genre.

Lauren Knoke

# Be in Charge of Your Reading Goal: Sign Up for Goal-Focused Small Groups

**Strategy** Read about the different types of reading groups around the classroom. Decide which group will best support you with what you want to work on as a reader. Sign up!

**What it is** In goal-setting conferences, I help students arrive at their own goals by leading them through questioning to discover what will be most important to work on. (For more information on goal-setting conferences, see Part IV of *Understanding Texts & Readers* and/or the sample video in the Online Resources.) The more students have a say in the work that they do in the classroom, the more likely they are to be invested, motivated, and engaged.

**How I'd teach it** You can offer strategy lessons by asking students to sign up for what they think would most help them. One way to offer options is to hang up signs around the classroom, each with a simple, kid-friendly definition of each of the possible goals, or "I" statements, and students can decide which one they identify with most. For example, for the goal of determining the main idea you might say, "This is a great goal for anyone who finds that they need help putting all the information in the text together to make one statement saying what the text is mostly about." For more "I" statements connected to reading goals, download a copy of the What Can I Work On as a Reader? self-reflection form from the Online Resources.

## Who is this for?

**LEVELS**
J–W

**SKILLS**
focus, stamina

*What Can I Work On as a Reader?* A Self-Reflection Tool for Finding Goals

Name: _____  Date: _____

| | Yes/Always | Kind of/ Sometimes | No/Never |
|---|---|---|---|
| **READING ENGAGEMENT** I have an easy time getting settled to read. | | | |
| I read for the entire time without distraction. | | | |
| I can easily find books I love that are a good fit. | | | |
| I love to read. | | | |
| **MAIN IDEA** When I read nonfiction, I can put together all the information to figure out (a) main idea(s). | | | |
| I can say what a chapter or section is mostly about. | | | |
| **KEY DETAILS** I understand and remember the important information that connects to a main idea. | | | |
| I can list the facts I learn. | | | |
| I pay attention to information/facts/details in what I read, and from text features in the book. | | | |
| **VOCABULARY** I am curious about words and what they mean. | | | |
| When I find words or phrases that are new, I try to figure out what they mean. | | | |
| I can often figure out what words and phrases mean. | | | |
| **TEXT FEATURES** I'm always sure to read and look closely at text features. | | | |
| I have a good understanding of how information from text features fits with the rest of the information on the page. | | | |

To download a copy of this form, visit the Online Resources.

# Main Idea

As Richard Allington writes in *What Really Matters for Struggling Readers* (2001), being able to summarize the main points of a text is "perhaps the most common and most necessary" skill to use when reading nonfiction because it helps students develop an understanding and remember what's been read (136). Although authors of lower-level books might make the main idea clear by announcing it in a heading or topic sentence, higher-level books often require the reader to do some thinking work. To determine main idea(s) in a more complex book, a reader must grapple with all the bits of information in a text (main text and text features), synthesize them or put them together, and distill the most important point(s) into a coherent sentence. This process often requires inference.

The reader also needs to determine the most important and most prevalent ideas in a section, a chapter, or the whole book, and must avoid being distracted by some "cool" fact that is only remotely connected to the main idea(s).

## Synthesizing and Inferring to Determine the Main Idea(s) of a Page, Section, or Chapter

It's important for readers to be able to synthesize information across a portion of a text, determine what details are related, and name the main idea(s). At Levels J–L, a reader can find a heading or topic sentence that contains the main idea and quote or paraphrase that heading or sentence. At Levels M–S, a reader will need to synthesize all the details within a given part and state a main idea in their own words. Beyond Level S, the main idea statement a reader crafts will be in original language and should communicate the complexity of the idea and take into account varied perspectives which are likely to be in the text. Across all levels, you should look to see how much of the text the reader is taking into account, and whether they are using both the main text and the text features or focusing only on one or the other.

## Synthesizing and Inferring to Determine the Main Idea(s) of a Whole Book

Students also need to be able to synthesize information across an entire text, determine what details are related, and name the main idea(s). This work often requires inference, as whole-book main ideas are rarely stated, though they may be hinted at through the title and/or if the book includes an introduction or conclusion. Beginning at Level O, a reader will need to start to see some complexity in the main idea. By Level R, they need to be able to recognize the breadth of information and state two or three important ideas of the whole text. At this level and beyond, students can be taught to state one complex overarching main idea (almost like a thesis statement) with several supporting main ideas that connect to it.

# Strategies for Determining Main Idea at a Glance

| Strategy | Levels | Skills | Page |
|---|---|---|---|
| MI.1 Picture It | J–M | Synthesizing and inferring to determine the main idea(s) of a page, section, or chapter | 32 |
| MI.2 What and So What | J–W | Synthesizing and inferring to determine the main idea(s) of a page, section, or chapter | 33 |
| MI.3 Find the Same (or Similar) Words and/or Phrases | J–W | Synthesizing and inferring to determine the main idea(s) of a page, section, or chapter | 34 |
| MI.4 Understand Clever Headings | J–W | Synthesizing and inferring to determine the main idea(s) of a page, section, or chapter | 35 |
| MI.5 From Question to Idea | J–W | Synthesizing and inferring to determine the main idea(s) of a page, section, or chapter | 36 |
| MI.6 Teach It | J–W | Synthesizing and inferring to determine the main idea(s) of a page, section, or chapter | 37 |
| MI.7 List Facts, Declare the Idea | M–W | Synthesizing and inferring to determine the main idea(s) of a page, section, or chapter | 38 |
| MI.8 Understand the Relationship Between Sentences | M–W | Synthesizing and inferring to determine the main idea(s) of a page, section, or chapter | 39 |
| MI.9 Text-Feature Addition | M–W | Synthesizing and inferring to determine the main idea(s) of a page, section, or chapter | 40 |
| MI.10 Build the Puzzle | M–W | Synthesizing and inferring to determine the main idea(s) of a page, section, or chapter | 41 |
| MI.11 Ignore the Distractors | M–W | Synthesizing and inferring to determine the main idea(s) of a page, section, or chapter | 42 |
| MI.12 Look Out for Words That Angle | M–W | Synthesizing and inferring to determine the main idea(s) of a page, section, or chapter | 43 |
| MI.13 Show and Tell | M–W | Synthesizing and inferring to determine the main idea(s) of a page, section, or chapter | 44 |
| MI.14 Use Your Words But the Author's Idea | M–W | Synthesizing and inferring to determine the main idea(s) of a page, section, or chapter | 45 |
| MI.15 Scan the Table of Contents | J–W | Synthesizing and inferring to determine the main idea(s) of a page, section, or chapter; synthesizing and inferring to determine the main idea(s) of a whole book | 46 |

# Strategies for Determining Main Idea at a Glance

# MI.1 Picture It

## Who is this for?

**LEVELS**

J–M

**SKILLS**

synthesizing and inferring to determine the main idea(s) of a page, section, or chapter

**Strategy** Look at a collection of objects, or a set of images. Think, "What are *most* of these about?" State a topic or idea.

**What it is** If the concept of a main idea seems challenging, you might start with a visual approach. Using everyday objects or images of things that are familiar to students can help them to see commonalities and practice making main idea statements.

**How I'd teach it** In their book *Navigating Nonfiction* (2010), Lucy Calkins and Kathleen Tolan recommend making a picture collage to support main idea instruction. In the collage, you could include pictures from magazines that go together in some way (i.e., a pendant necklace, a bracelet, earrings, a string of pearls), as well as a few items that don't (a piece of pizza and a chair). Then ask students to look at the collage and say what most—not necessarily all—of the pictures relate to.

**Tip** This strategy is best for coming up with a topic or basic idea.

# What and So What

**Strategy** First name the topic of the text (the "What") and then what the author has to say about that topic (the "So What").

**What it is** Determining a main idea is more than just being able to name the topic. It also requires being able to identify the author's angle on, or idea about, the topic. This can be hard for students, and I've found giving them lots of examples helps. You might also consider maintaining an ongoing class chart of main ideas you discover over time.

**How I'd teach it** For example, if the topic, or "What," is women on the home front during World War II, the main idea, or "So What," could be "Women's entry into the U.S. workforce was essential to our country's success in the war." If the topic is Iroquois clothing, the main idea could be "The Iroquois always made use of an entire animal after hunting, including for their clothing." When doing this work, readers could ask themselves, "What is the author trying to say about this topic? That it's interesting? That it's scary? That it's misunderstood?" The topic plus the author's angle—or what the author seems to care most about—is the main idea.

*Who is this for?*

**LEVELS**

J–W

**SKILLS**

synthesizing and inferring to determine the main idea(s) of a page, section, or chapter

Main Ideas

**Tip:** Name the topic— the "What."

State what the author has to say about the topic. —the "So What."

| Topic: the "What." | Main Idea: the "So What." |
|---|---|
| Honeybees | Bees are social creatures. |
| Dolphins | Dolphins are highly intelligent. |
| Bats | Bats are often misunderstood. |

Marjorie Martinelli

# MI.3

# Find the Same (or Similar) Words and/or Phrases

## Who is this for?

### LEVELS
J–W

### SKILLS
synthesizing and inferring to determine the main idea(s) of a page, section, or chapter

**Strategy** Take note of words and phrases (or synonyms) that show up again and again in a section. Reread the sentences where those repeated words appear. Use the topic of the section plus that repeated word or phrase to state a main idea as a sentence.

**What it is** The main idea is what the text is *mostly* about. This will likely mean that it is described by a word or phrase that shows up more than once in the text. So readers should be on the lookout for that word or phrase. They should also be on the lookout for synonymous words and phrases that could illuminate the main idea.

**How I'd teach it** In *Finding the Titanic* by Robert Ballard (1993), Chapter 2 includes a word bank of synonyms for *big* ("huge," "11-story," "largest," "tall," "walk for miles," "grand"). Those words act as clues to the main idea of the chapter: the Titanic was an enormous ship that included many features.

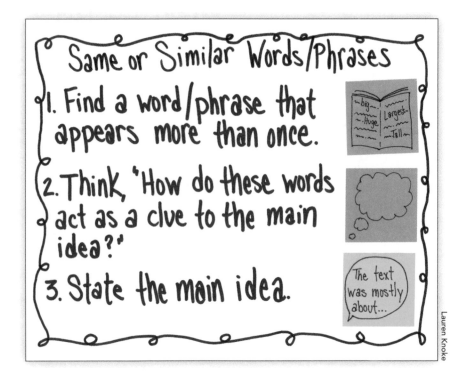

Same or Similar Words/Phrases
1. Find a word/phrase that appears more than once.
2. Think, "How do these words act as a clue to the main idea?"
3. State the main idea.

Lauren Knoke

# Understand Clever Headings

**Strategy**  Study a heading. Think, "How does this heading connect to the main idea of the book? What might this section be about?" State the possible main idea, and read the section to confirm or revise.

**What it is**  Sometimes headings in nonfiction texts clearly announce the main idea, and sometimes they don't. When headings are clever and crafty, readers need to slow down and stop and think to make sure they understand the text and its main idea(s).

**How I'd teach it**  For example, in an article on snakes, a reader might come to a section called "Smooth Move"—which doesn't announce the main idea. The reader might think it has something to do with movement, and connect it to the whole article about snakes. Then, reading on, the reader might learn that although snakes appear slick, most have rough skin that helps them move.

*Who is this for?*

LEVELS
J–W

SKILLS

synthesizing and inferring to determine the main idea(s) of a page, section, or chapter

 **MI.5**

# From Question to Idea

**Strategy**  Read the heading. Read the section, and then go back to the heading to turn it from a question into a statement.

---

**What it is**  Headings that are written as questions can help focus the reader, but can be tricky when it comes to naming the main idea because readers will need to use original language.

---

**How I'd teach it**  In *How Do Frogs Swallow with Their Eyes?* by Melvin and Gilda Berger (2002a), the heading reads, "Do amphibians have good senses of smell and taste?" (14). After reading the section and learning the information, students would need to go back and state an appropriate main idea based on what they read. The facts they read can help them answer the question. Will the main idea be "Amphibians need their senses of smell and taste to survive" or "Smell and taste are the weakest of all of an amphibian's senses"?

Step 1: Read the HEADING

Do amphibians have a good sense of smell + taste?

Step 2: Read the SECTION

• smell not used to detect food

• can sense changes in chemicals in air!

Step 3: Turn the QUESTION into a STATEMENT

Sense of smell + taste is used in surprising ways.

# Teach It

**Strategy** Pause after reading a section, and teach your partner what you learned. After listing out the information and facts think, "So based on what I have just said, what does it seem like this section is mostly about?" Teach your partner.

**What it is** Teaching about their topic, or talking through it, can help readers articulate a main idea. When you have to teach something, you often endeavor to learn and understand it better. You can't just get the gist; you need to know it well to explain it to someone else.

**How I'd teach it** In a small-group or whole-class lesson focused on the main idea, you might consider using a short video clip such as a five-minute documentary from the BBC or National Geographic. (A quick search on YouTube will yield many options.) While showing the clip, you can pause periodically and say to students, "Assume your partner hasn't just watched what you saw. Can you turn to teach your partner what you just learned?" After watching the entire clip, you could ask readers to then think with a partner about all the facts they taught to their partner, and then put that information together to name the main idea of the clip. Access a recorded sample lesson using a video clip in the Online Resources.

Kelly Boyle

## Who is this for?

**LEVELS**

J–W

**SKILLS**

synthesizing and inferring to determine the main idea(s) of a page, section, or chapter

# MI.7

# List Facts, Declare the Idea

*Who is this for?*

**LEVELS**

M–W

**SKILLS**

synthesizing and inferring to determine the main idea(s) of a page, section, or chapter

**Strategy**  After reading a section, list out important facts. Then think, "Which of these facts are related? How are they related?" How the facts fit together explains what the text is mostly about. State a main idea in your own words.

**What it is**  Many people fit into one of two categories: part-to-whole thinkers or whole-to-part thinkers. A whole-to-part thinker is the kind of person who, after watching a movie, might tell you about it in a sentence or two: "This is another one of those rags-to-riches stories." A part-to-whole thinker, on the other hand, might start retelling scenes in the story, and then at the end of their retelling say, "So, you know, it's one of those rags-to-riches stories." Teach students who are part-to-whole thinkers to list facts first, and then declare the main idea. They can do this on a sticky note or in a notebook immediately after reading.

**How I'd teach it**  Using Paul Coco's "Hip Hoppers" (2004), an article about frogs, you might list the following facts from the section "Hopping Helpers" as you model:

- Eighty poison-dart species live in Central and South America.

- Some frogs have chemicals in their skin that can be used to make medicine.

- When deformed frogs are found, it's often a sign that the environment is dangerous, which can compel people to make changes before people are hurt.

Have students look back across the facts you wrote and consider how they relate and then model your thinking by saying, "Which of these facts are related? How are they related? Well, the first one is about how many frogs there are in Central and South America. The other two are about how they are useful to people, so maybe the main idea of this section—what most sentences are about—is: 'Frogs can sometimes be a big help to humans.' That matches the heading, 'Hopping Helpers,' and it's similar to the topic sentence."

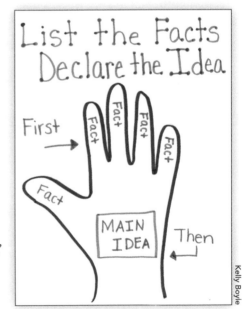

Kelly Boyle

# Understand the Relationship Between Sentences

**Strategy** Read an entire paragraph or section. Ask yourself, "Which sentence seems to make a broad statement about the whole section? Which sentences seem to support that statement?" Reread to understand the relationship between the sentences.

**What it is** A topic sentence in a paragraph or section contains a main idea, usually appearing at the very beginning or end of the section, but sometimes found tucked in the middle of a section. These sentences are often overlooked by readers or misunderstood as just one sentence among many. If we can clue readers in to the importance of topic sentences as holders of main ideas, we will help them read with more purpose and understanding.

**How I'd teach it** Alert readers to the places where topic sentences may be found, discouraging them from assuming it's always the first sentence.

For example, the very first sentence of each section of Kevin Holmes' *Sharks* (1998) is the topic sentence, making it easy for the reader to ascertain the main idea of each section. For example, on page 11, the section titled "Strengths" begins: "A shark is a powerful predator." The details that follow support this idea: "Some sharks can bite 300 times harder than people," "An adult shark replaces its outer set of teeth seven to 12 times each year," and "The scales help protect the shark."

Barbara Golub

# MI.9

# Text-Feature Addition

## Who is this for?

### LEVELS

M–W

### SKILLS

synthesizing and inferring to determine the main idea(s) of a page, section, or chapter

**Strategy**  Study a section or page spread. Look around the pages from feature to feature, thinking, "How do all of these features fit together?" Think about what the main idea of the section might be. Then read the rest of the page and revise based on what you read.

**What it is**  A reader of nonfiction can view each section of nonfiction text as an addition problem. It is important to study each part of the section—the pictures, diagrams, captions, and so forth—and add them together to come up with the main idea. In this sense, the main idea is like the grand total.

**How I'd teach it**  In Rebecca Stanborough's *The Golden Gate Bridge* (2016), the section "Construction Begins" features historical photographs of men standing in a long line for jobs, a man walking on a partially completed bridge being blown about by the wind, and Skid Row, where San Francisco's poor and unemployed lived. A reader could scan these features and add them up to come up with a possible main idea, "The workers who constructed the bridge were desperate for work, even if it was dangerous."

**Tip**  This is a great idea for partnership time, or for incorporating into interactive read-aloud or video-aloud lessons, as it invites conversation. During discussions, children could list the information they are learning and talk about how it may all fit together. Have them phrase and rephrase main idea statements, and get feedback from peers about whether their word choices are true to information in the book.

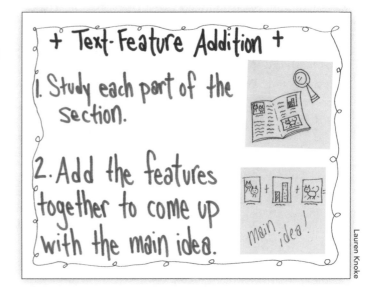

+ Text-Feature Addition +

1. Study each part of the section.

2. Add the features together to come up with the main idea.

main idea!

Lauren Knoke

# Build the Puzzle

**Strategy** As you read each sentence ask, "How does this detail fit with the others I have just read?" As you read, visualize putting the details together, like pieces of a puzzle.

**What it is** When students are reading nonfiction, it is essential that they see the interrelatedness of details.

**How I'd teach it** You might consider reading aloud part of a page from Seymour Simon's *Gorillas* (2009): "Gorillas spend much of the day feeding in open, sunny sections of the forest that are just growing back after a fire or a storm. When feeding, gorillas space themselves out so that they are not on top of one another. They eat juicy fruits, leaves, stems, and shoots" (19). "Hmm. This seems to be telling me where gorillas feed and what they eat. Let me read on to see if other details support that idea: 'A 400-pound gorilla can eat up to 50 pounds of plants a day. The plants contain so much water that gorillas rarely need open water for drinking.' Yes, this is about how much food they eat and why they eat certain foods. How do all of these details fit together? They connect to food. So, I think this part is about gorillas' eating habits."

Merridy Gnagey

# MI.11

# Ignore the Distractors

*Who is this for?*

**LEVELS**

M–W

**SKILLS**

synthesizing and inferring to determine the main idea(s) of a page, section, or chapter

**Strategy**  As you read each sentence, caption, or bolded fact, ask yourself, "How does this fit with what the section is mostly about? How does this fit together with the other information I've read?" Be aware that sometimes the topic relates only to the other facts but not the main idea.

**What it is**  Some nonfiction books contain eye-catching graphics, varied fonts, boxed facts, and other text features that can make it harder to identify the main idea.

**How I'd teach it**  Author/photographer Nic Bishop has a tendency to set sentences containing cool details in bold, enlarged type so they pop out. However, those sentences do not necessarily connect to the section's main idea. So readers must ask, "How do all these details fit together?" One page in Bishop's *Spiders* (2007) reads like this: "Some spiders are as small as a grain of sand. **The biggest, the Goliath birdeater tarantula from South America, is as big as a page in this book**. Yet all spiders share similar features. They have eight legs, fangs, spin silk, and eat other animals. At first you might confuse them with insects. But it is easy to tell the difference. Insects have six legs; spiders have eight. And spiders never have wings" (8, bold text formatting original to the book). A reader might be tempted to say that the main idea has something to do with the Goliath birdeater tarantula, because of the bolded text, when in fact that statement isn't even a supporting detail. The main idea might sound like this: "You can tell if something is a spider because all spiders have certain things in common."

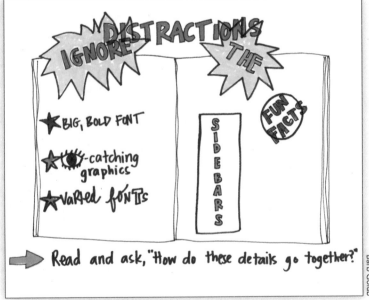

Barb Golub

# Look Out for Words That Angle

**Strategy** Be on the lookout for opinion words as you read. When you see one, think, "How does the author feel about this topic? How is the author trying to make me feel?" Read on to see if the information included in the section confirms that slant. Use the author's opinion to help you state the main idea(s).

**What it is** Many of us think authors of informational texts are impartial. But many texts are written with a bias or slant. Or they lure us in by providing an opinion on a topic. We can teach students to be on the lookout for hints about the author's opinion.

**How I'd teach it** In Melvin and Gilda Berger's *Ugly Animals* (2011b), each section is about a particular animal that the authors consider ugly. They use words such as *bizarre*, *clumsy*, *strange*, and *scary* to describe the animals. Read this book aloud, pausing after each of those words to ask students how the authors are trying to make them feel about the animals. For example, "The Aye-Aye is so-o-o ugly. It has large, staring eyes, and ears that look much too big for its body. And its fingers are as thin as wires" (18). Think aloud here: "I read the phrases *so-o-o ugly*, *staring eyes*, *ears much too big*. I'm thinking that the authors must believe that the Aye-Aye is strange-looking. That opinion helps me state the main idea of this section." Modeling this strategy reinforces the fact that not everything in a nonfiction book is a fact.

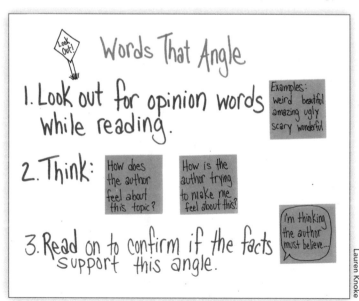

# MI.13    Show and Tell

## Who is this for?

**LEVELS**

M–W

**SKILLS**

synthesizing and inferring to determine the main idea(s) of a page, section, or chapter

**Strategy**   Read one fact. Repeat it in your own words. Ask yourself, "What does this fact show about the topic of this section? What does that mean the main idea might be?"

**What it is**   If you're working with a speedy reader who jumps from fact to fact without noticing what bigger idea might knit facts together, this strategy might help them.

**How I'd teach it**   For example, if a student is reading the *Scholastic News* article "Kids on the Battlefield," the main idea may not be immediately obvious because the title states only the topic, not the idea. The title of the article's first section is "A Nation Divided"—still a topic (the Civil War), not a main idea. A reader might continue further to read the facts, "From 1861 to 1865, Americans fought a bloody war against each other. It was a war that affected entire American families. Even many kids were involved. Some were as young as nine years old." At this point, a teacher might coach the child to stop and think about what all the facts taught him or her. The student might respond, "I learned that the Civil War was a terrible time for Americans of all ages. So the main idea of the article might be that even children played an important part in the Civil War."

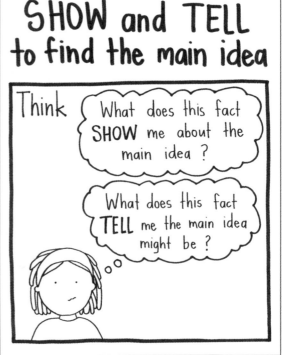

Merridy Gnagey

# Use Your Words But the Author's Idea

**Strategy** Find a sentence or couple of sentences that capture the main idea of the section. Use synonyms for the words the author's using to change the way the sentence is phrased, while still holding true to the idea.

**What it is** In *Comprehension Through Conversation* (2006), Maria Nichols discusses the importance of students using their own words to aid their comprehension.

**How I'd teach it** In Russell Freedman's *Immigrant Kids* (1980), you may read aloud: "In the years around the turn of the century, immigration to America reached an all-time high. Between 1880 and 1920, 23 million immigrants arrived in the United States. They came mainly from the countries of Europe, especially the impoverished towns and villages in southern and eastern Europe. The one thing they had in common was a fervent belief that in America, life would be better" (4). Think aloud about how there are some challenging words in the text that may be difficult to include in a main idea statement. Instead, tell students they should try using their own words. *All-time high* in my own words might be *a lot*. *Impoverished* might be *poor*. When stating the main idea for this section of *Immigrant Kids*, readers should try to use their own language. To synthesize in my own words the main parts and capture the main idea that the author is trying to communicate, I might say, "There were lots of poor European immigrants who came to America in search of a better life."

Barb Golub

*Who is this for?*

**LEVELS**
M–W

**SKILLS**
synthesizing and inferring to determine the main idea(s) of a page, section, or chapter

# MI.15 Scan the Table of Contents

## Who is this for?

**LEVELS**
J–W

**SKILLS**
synthesizing and inferring to determine the main idea(s) of a page, section, or chapter; synthesizing and inferring to determine the main idea(s) of a whole book

**Strategy** Scan the table of contents. Think, "What will I learn in each chapter/section? What is the whole book mostly about?"

**What it is** Scanning the table of contents can be a useful way to preview a book before reading it to grasp its main idea(s). It also can be a useful way to help a reader learn and remember the book's big topics.

**How I'd teach it** If you're reading *You Wouldn't Want to Live in Pompeii* by John Malam (2008), you could think aloud or even have students think through how the sections fit together around a main idea. "Let's look through the table of contents. Hmm. I see 'Earthquake!,' 'Flashback to AD 62,' 'Little Bang! Vesuvius Wakes Up,' 'Big Bang! Vesuvius Blows Its Top,' and 'Panic! Pompeii in Chaos.' These sections all seem to be about disasters in Pompeii. That makes me think that the main idea of the whole book could be that Pompeii is a city that has endured much destruction."

**Tip** Spend some time comparing the tables of contents in nonfiction books. Notice how some authors title a chapter with just the topic, while others use a phrase that hints at the main idea. Still others use clever wordplay that only remotely connects to the topic or main idea. Tell students that even when the author doesn't announce a main idea, they should be thinking about it (see the strategy titled Understand Clever Headings on page 35 for more help with this).

Kelly Boyle

# Act Like an Expert

**Strategy**  As you read, keep in mind that you'll meet with a partner to teach them about what you've read. Prepare to collect facts so they fit together. As you read, think, "What's the big thing I'm trying to teach my partner?"

**What it is**  When partners get together to discuss books, you can hold them accountable for understanding what they've read by having them teach it to one another. This summarizing also will help students remember and better understand their reading.

**How I'd teach it**  Sometimes when readers meet in partnerships, they are inclined to share cool facts, pictures, and other minutiae that detract from the overall meaning of the book. You might consider creating a chart to keep partnerships focused. It could include guiding questions such as these:

- What's most important about my topic?
- What's the most important main idea I want to teach about this topic?
- What can I teach my partner about this main idea?
- What does the author want me to think/feel/believe about my topic?

Kristine Mraz

**Who is this for?**

**LEVELS**

M–W

**SKILLS**

synthesizing and inferring to determine the main idea(s) of a page, section, or chapter; synthesizing and inferring to determine the main idea(s) of a whole book

# MI.17

# Digest Instead of List

## LEVELS

M–W

## SKILLS

synthesizing and inferring to determine the main idea(s) of a page, section, or chapter; synthesizing and inferring to determine the main idea(s) of a whole book

**Strategy** Slow down as you read and check for understanding as you go by thinking, "This sentence was mostly about. . . ." Before continuing to the next sentence, see if you can name a way that all the facts go together so far.

**What it is** Sometimes readers approach nonfiction in the same way they approach fiction. They expect to read it quickly and fall into the world of the book. But nonfiction reading should be slower. Information can be dense and readers often need time to digest it.

**How I'd teach it** Nic Bishop's *Butterflies and Moths* (2009) contains no headings, so readers must read each sentence and see if they can name a way in which all the facts go together. For example, page 10 reads, "The life of a butterfly or moth begins with an egg, no bigger than a grain of sand. This egg may look like a ball, a barrel, or a saucer. It may have been laid alone or with a group of eggs. Some butterflies lay their eggs on top of each other, like stacks of tiny teacups. About a week after it is laid, each egg will have a tiny dot inside, and the dot will be moving. With a hand lens, you will see that the dot is the head of a caterpillar, chewing a hole to wriggle its way out." Pause and read sentence by sentence, thinking aloud about how they go together around a main idea: "The life of a butterfly or moth begins with an egg, no bigger than a grain of sand." "Hmm. Butterfly eggs are small. Maybe this section is mostly about size. Let me read on to check. 'This egg may look like a ball, a barrel, or a saucer.' Hmm. They can be shaped like balls, barrels, or saucers. Now it seems to be about shape. I'm going to keep reading to find a bigger idea that shows how details overlap. 'It may have been laid alone or with a group of eggs. Some butterflies lay their eggs on top of each other, like stacks of tiny teacups.' This sentence is about how and where eggs are laid. I'm thinking that all of these sentences are about eggs. What about the eggs? 'Eggs—in a variety of shapes and sizes—are the beginning of the butterfly and moth life cycle.'"

Digest Instead of List

1. Pause after each sentence.

2. Think, "This sentence was mostly about..."

3. Name a way all the facts go together.

I'm thinking that all of these sentences are about...

Lauren Kroke

# Put Your Own Ideas Aside

## MI.18

**Strategy** Be open-minded when approaching a text. Focus on the facts that are on the page, rather than your own assumptions about the topic. Think, "What does the author say about this topic?"

**What it is** Sometimes readers approach a text with preconceived notions. It is imperative that readers have the ability to separate their personal biases and opinions from the facts in a text.

**How I'd teach it** In James Solheim's *It's Disgusting and We Ate It!* (1998) there is a section entitled "Earthworm Soup" (4). It discusses how earthworm soup was used as an ancient medicine and was a sign of royalty. It could be a problem if readers focus on their initial opinion: earthworm soup is disgusting! They need to take in new information and think, "What does the author say about this topic?" Questions such as "What details in the text led you to this idea?" will help keep readers focused.

Similarly, a reader might approach a text about child soldiers in the Civil War with preconceived notions and say, "I can't believe a nine-year-old boy would want to lie about his age to join the army. He'd be putting his life at risk for nothing." But when approaching the text, the reader needs to be ready to determine the author's point of view. Details like "Many of them wanted to be with their fathers and brothers," and "Officers depended on drummer boys to bang out their commands as drumbeats," might prompt students to say, "Although I think it's wrong to have kids fight in wars, I can see how the drummer boys played an important part in the battlefields of the Civil War."

Who is this for?

**LEVELS**
M–W

**SKILLS**

synthesizing and inferring to determine the main idea(s) of a page, section, or chapter; synthesizing and inferring to determine the main idea(s) of a whole book

Merridy Gnagey

# MI.19    Look for Shifts

## Who is this for?

**LEVELS**

M–W

**SKILLS**

synthesizing and inferring to determine the main idea(s) of a whole book

**Strategy** As you read, create your own headings if the book doesn't have them, at the start of each new part. Notice a place where the subtopic shifts to a new subtopic by continuously thinking, "Is this fact related to the last one or does it connect with a new idea?"

**What it is** Headings announce a change of topic or subtopic. So when students are reading a book without them, they need to be ready to shift their thinking when a new topic or subtopic occurs.

**How I'd teach it** Often titles can be deceiving. Take the book *What Do You Do with a Tail Like This?* by Steve Jenkins and Robin Page (2003). The title alone highlights tails. Perhaps readers would infer the main idea of the text has something to do with animal tails. However, the book is structured in sections which shift from one animal body part to another. Readers should be on the lookout for these shifts. For example, the first section is about animal noses and their many functions, and the second section focuses on ears and how they allow animals to adapt to their environment.

# Add Up Headings

**Strategy**  While reading a book without headings, you can jot your own heading on a sticky note, at the end of each section or spread. Then, lay these sticky notes out on a table, and ask yourself, "How do all these subtopics seem to fit together? What is the main idea of the whole book? What is the author saying about that idea?"

**What it is**  Just as readers can add up facts within a section to determine the main idea, they can add up headings to determine the main idea of a whole book. These can be headings that the author has created, or headings that students themselves create.

**How I'd teach it**  This strategy can be adapted for students who create their own headings on sticky notes (as shown in the image below, and as described in the previous strategy, Look for Shifts) and it can also be adapted to work with students who finish a portion of text that has many headings. In that case, readers can be directed to go back through the book, rereading the headings to each section, while thinking, "How do all of these headings fit together?"

**Who is this for?**

**LEVELS**
M–W

**SKILLS**

synthesizing and inferring to determine the main idea(s) of a whole book

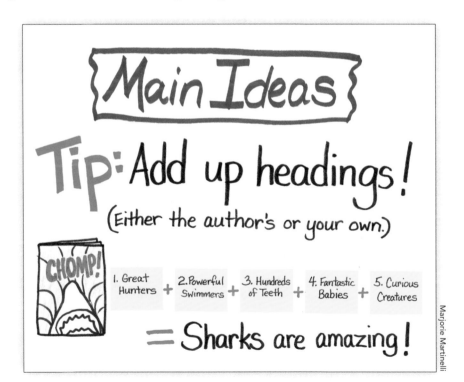

Marjorie Martinelli

# MI.21 Read the Introduction Carefully

## Who is this for?

**LEVELS**

M–W

**SKILLS**

synthesizing and inferring to determine the main idea(s) of a whole book

**Strategy** Read the introduction, pause, and think: "What does it seem like this whole book is likely to be about? What information does the introduction set me up to learn about?"

**What it is** Sometimes students skip over the page that introduces the book's main idea or ideas to the first cool-looking page.

**How I'd teach it** Take Seymour Simon's *Animals Nobody Loves* (2001). At first glance, the reader may think that the main idea is simply the title: animals nobody loves. However, the introduction reveals more: "Some animals just have bad reputations that are not based on fact. Animals are not bad or evil. They do what they must in order to survive." After you have read the introduction, you can highlight that last sentence, "They do what they must in order to survive," by asking students, "What is the introduction telling us about animals nobody loves?" With this idea from the introduction in mind, readers are more likely to bring each section of the book—those about sharks, bats, grizzly bears, cobras, and so forth—back to the main idea: that each animal does what it must to survive. Had the reader skipped the introduction, that vital, unifying idea would have been missed—and finding the main idea would have required a lot more work!

Read ALLLLL the Parts:

1. Turn to the INTRODUCTION.

2. READ IT.

3. Pause and think:

"What does it seem like this WHOLE BOOK is likely to be about?"

"What information does the INTRODUCTION set me up to learn?"

# Picture Walk Before, During, and After Reading

**Strategy** Use visuals as tools to help you summarize the whole book's main idea or ideas. Preview them before you read, notice them as you read, and revisit them after reading to remember key information. When looking at the visuals, think, "What is the main topic of this book? Based on what's in the pictures and illustrations, what is the angle on the topic?"

**What it is** If you watch students read an informational text, sometimes you'll see them ignore visuals, such as pictures, opting instead to focus on just the text; or you'll see eyes darting back and forth between visuals and words, referring to those visuals while reading. This strategy serves as a helpful reminder of the usefulness of visual information in nonfiction, and offers advice for how to use visuals before, during, and after reading to think about the main idea(s).

**How I'd teach it** This lesson idea could really be three separate strategies: one for teaching children how to use images in previewing the text's main idea(s), another lesson about using the visuals during the reading of the text, and a third about revisiting visuals to remember key information that may be useful in synthesizing the information. For previewing, you might use *Through My Eyes: Ruby Bridges* by Margo Lundell (1999) as an example of just how useful pictures can be. You may choose to preview the book solely by taking a picture walk, or you might decide to focus on and analyze a few photographs. Then, as you read the text, ask children to continue checking pictures with the prompt: "Based on the pictures, what is the main idea of the text?"

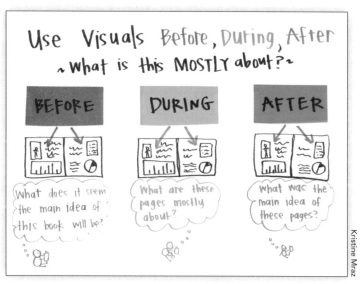

Kristine Mraz

# MI.23

# Read the Conclusion Carefully

**LEVELS**

M–W

**SKILLS**

synthesizing and inferring to determine the main idea(s) of a whole book

**Strategy**  Reread the final section, or last paragraphs, of a nonfiction book. Ask yourself, "How did those sentences sum up what the book is really about?"

**What it is**  Often, the last words in a nonfiction book—the words at the very end, are designed to leave the reader lingering over an important point—reveal its main idea. These conclusions are often written with weighted words that indicate the author's slant or perspective.

**How I'd teach it**  In *Animal Dads* (1997), Sneed Collard leaves the reader with the words, "Dads do many things. Dads are many things." These two sentences capture the main idea of the entire text by threading all the vignettes in the book together.

If you are conferring with a reader who has just completed a nonfiction text, you may want to say, "Nonfiction writers sometimes end their books by giving away the main idea. At times, you can read or reread those last sentences, and the main idea is right there! Let's see if we can uncover the main idea by using this strategy." Consider having the student reread the last few sentences from the book before asking, "How did those sentences summarize what the book was really about?"

Lauren Knoke

# Consider Overall Structure

**Strategy**  Consider how the text is organized. Think: "Is the text divided into sections, each section forming part of a bigger idea? Is the author comparing and contrasting more than one thing? Is the author teaching about the cause-and-effect relationship between two things? Is it written as a narrative?" The way the information is organized can help readers uncover main idea(s).

**What it is**  The main idea may relate to the structure of the text. For example, if the text is structured in a way that invites the reader to compare and contrast two topics or ideas, the main idea should take into account both. If a reader only refers to one of the topics or ideas, the main idea is likely to be incomplete.

**How I'd teach it**  Take Melvin and Gilda Berger's *True or False: Mammals* (2011a). The main idea can be stated by rephrasing the title: there are many truths and misconceptions about mammals. Each section of the book acts as a supporting detail: some explain a truth about mammals, some explain misconceptions. If students do not take time to familiarize themselves with the structure, they could miss out on the main idea.

*Who is this for?*

LEVELS
M–W

SKILLS

synthesizing and inferring to determine the main idea(s) of a whole book

| Know the STRUCTURE | To do the THINKING |
|---|---|
| Compare & contrast | consider both topics and /or ideas |
| narrative | think about the ~~theme / idea / lesson~~ you could learn |
| sections | find how each part is part of a bigger idea |
| X → Y cause & effect | notice the reasons something happened |

Barb Golub

# MI.25

# Test the Idea with Proof

## Who is this for?

### LEVELS

O–W

### SKILLS

synthesizing and inferring to determine the main idea(s) of a page, section, or chapter

**Strategy**  After a first read of a section, state what you think is the main idea. Go back through the section and list facts that you believe prove that main idea. If you have many, you likely have stated a main idea that works with the text. If you don't have many, think about how you might revise the main idea.

**What it is**  A main idea must be supported by proof from the text. When reading an informational text, we can test what we think to be the main idea by gathering a number of details that support it: the proof. Readers can practice this alone or with a partner.

**How I'd teach it**  Using Melvin Berger's *Chomp! A Book About Sharks* (1999) to model for a small group how to find the main idea, I might begin by offering the main idea and then making sure I have enough details to prove that idea. I might model after reading a page by saying, "I think the main idea for this section is that swimming is an important part of a shark's life. But I should have plenty of details to support it. Let's see how many I can find. I read that:

Marjorie Martinelli

- 'Sharks have sleek, rounded bodies that make swimming easy.'

- 'Fins keep sharks steady in the water.'

- 'Sharks can swim up to sixty miles per hour.'

- 'Sharks have to swim to breathe.'

- 'Swimming keeps the shark afloat.'

This idea seems like a main idea because I was able to find lots of support. From now on, you might try to list out details to support a main idea in order to be sure it is, in fact, a main idea."

# Pop-Out Sentences

**Strategy**  Read through a section of text. Consider each sentence and think, "Which one of these sentences seems to say what the text is mostly about, and which support that sentence? Which sentence seems to fit with the heading?" After finding the pop-out sentence, state the main idea in your own words.

**What it is**  In many nonfiction books, there are sentences that seem as if they should be written in bold because they contain words or phrases that angle toward the main idea. We can call these "pop-out sentences."

**How I'd teach it**  I've taught this strategy using Steve Jenkins' *Down Down Down* (2009). In the section "It's Snowing!" he writes, "We've reached the dark zone. Not even the faintest sunlight can reach us here. It's getting colder, and the pressure is enormous. Few submarines can dive this deep without being crushed. All around us a delicate 'marine snow' is falling. It's composed of dead plankton, fish scales, animal waste, and bits of larger creatures that have died in the waters above. These particles are the basis of life here. Small animals feed on marine snow and become prey for larger hunters." Sifting through the paragraph, the sentence that angles most toward the main idea is: "These particles are the basis of life here." When combined with the heading, "It's Snowing," the main idea might be something like this: "Marine snow is important in sustaining life at this depth in the ocean."

Notice **POP-OUT** Sentences...

Goes with heading...

All other sentences seem to fit...

Connects to the Main Idea...

Kelly Boyle

## Who is this for?

**LEVELS**

O–W

**SKILLS**

synthesizing and inferring to determine the main idea(s) of a page, section, or chapter

# MI.27 Look for Related Main Ideas

## LEVELS

P–W

## SKILLS

synthesizing and inferring to determine the main idea(s) of a whole book

**Strategy** Think about the topic of the whole text. Within each section, be prepared to learn about a different angle/idea about that topic. When you put them all together, think, "What's one overarching main idea, and what are the sub–main ideas that fit with it?"

**What it is** More complex texts, beginning around Level P, often have several related main ideas. A reader should be able to list the main ideas that relate to one overarching main idea.

**How I'd teach it** In *If You Lived in the Days of the Knights* by Ann McGovern (2001), the author offers details to support the main idea that castles were uncomfortable places to live: "Castles were damp and very cold" (26); "Small windows, covered with oiled cloth, did not let in much light" (26); "The floor was covered with straw that got dirty from spilled food and dog poop" (27). Later, the reader learns about the challenges people faced to keep clean: "they had no running water" (34); "You cleaned your teeth with a twig" (34); "soap was made at home, but it was smelly" (34). You could model for children how you can think about the sub-ideas together and state an overarching main idea such as "Life in the time of the knights had more challenges than it does today," or "During the time of the knights there were fewer comforts than today."

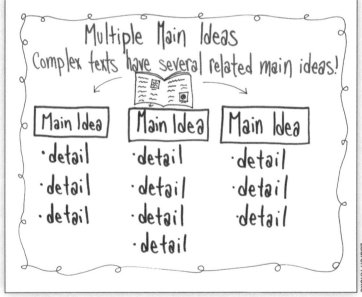

Lauren Knoke

# Jot After Each Section, Then Combine

## MI.28

**Strategy** After each section, you can jot on a sticky note the main idea of that section. Then, when you finish reading, you can look across all their notes and ask, "Adding all these ideas up, what seems to be the big thing or things I'm learning from this text?"

**What it is** We can teach readers to be note takers as they read—not of every little fact, but of the big ideas the author is putting forward.

**How I'd teach it** Consider the jots in the chart from the book *Owen and Mzee* by Craig Hatkoff, Isabella Hatkoff, and Paula Kahumbu (2006). A reader can look over the jots: "Villagers worked together to rescue the baby hippo," "The doctors tried to find ways to keep Owen calm," and "Mzee helped Owen adjust to life in the wildlife preserve." And after considering the jots, a reader can think, "Hmm. These jots represent the big ideas for each part of the book. If I add them together, what is the author trying to teach me? I think that the author is really trying to tell me that things work best when people and animals work together."

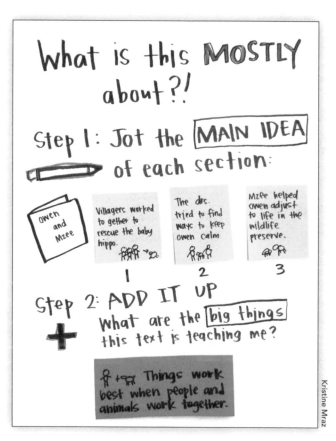

Kristine Mraz

## Skills That Enhance Determining Key Details

----------

Determining importance to support a main idea with key details from the text

Comparing and contrasting key details

# Key Details

Nonfiction texts are filled with information—both in the main text and in text features. As students read more challenging texts, the number of details they encounter grows. As readers, they will need to sort through all of that information to determine the difference between what is important, or "key," because it supports the text's main idea(s), and what information might be interesting, but is more extraneous to the main idea(s) in the text. They also need to understand how facts and information they read connect to other facts and information within the text.

## Determining Importance to Support a Main Idea with Key Details from the Text

Many of the strategies in this section help readers to distinguish details that are essential, because they support a main idea, from those that are more tangential.

At Levels J–O, readers need to support a main idea with several key details from many parts of a text, drawing on both words and pictures. At Levels P–R, as texts become longer and more information-filled, readers need to pull information from different sections or chapters, and from more complex text features. Beginning at Level S, readers need not only to identify details, but also to explain how they support the main idea, to show they understand why the author includes certain information within sections or chapters. By Level V, we can expect readers to do all that's been mentioned previously, plus use direct quotations in support of main ideas.

## Comparing and Contrasting Key Details

Understanding connections between key details is another important skill students need. To fully comprehend the text, they must be able to compare similarities among details and contrast differences.

Up to Level M, since texts offer few details within each section, readers should be able to compare or contrast two details. Beginning at Level M, a reader should be able to pinpoint multiple similarities and differences among key details to support a main idea. It is likely that readers will compare and contrast concepts, events, or facts that belong in the same category. They should be discouraged from summarizing and paraphrasing details and encouraged to use information directly from the text. Although the expectation remains the same for Levels M–W, as texts increase in complexity, readers will encounter many more key details, and those details will be more complex. Being able to understand how the information relates becomes increasingly challenging.

# Strategies for Determining Key Details at a Glance

# Strategies for Determining Key Details at a Glance

| Strategy | Levels | Skills | Page |
|---|---|---|---|
| KD.13  Go Outside the Book | J–W | Comparing and contrasting key details | 76 |
| KD.14  Speak the Language of Comparison | J–W | Comparing and contrasting key details | 77 |
| KD.15  Use Superlatives | J–W | Comparing and contrasting key details | 78 |
| KD.16  Think in Categories | M–W | Comparing and contrasting key details | 79 |
| KD.17  Identify a Compare-and-Contrast Structure | O–W | Comparing and contrasting key details | 80 |
| KD.18  Use a Venn Diagram or Three-Column Chart | O–W | Comparing and contrasting key details | 81 |
| KD.19  Compare Apples to Apples | O–W | Comparing and contrasting key details | 82 |
| KD.20  How Do These Parts Connect? | O–W | Comparing and contrasting key details | 83 |
| KD.21  Compare Perspectives | O–W | Comparing and contrasting key details | 84 |
| KD.22  Identifying Multiple Perspectives | O–W | Comparing and contrasting key details | 85 |
| KD.23  Compare Past and Present | O–W | Comparing and contrasting key details | 86 |
| KD.24  Compare Historical Figures and Their Perspectives | O–W | Comparing and contrasting key details | 87 |

# KD.1

# Sit Up and Pay Attention

## Who is this for?

### LEVELS

J–W

### SKILLS

determining importance to support a main idea with key details from the text

**Strategy** Pause after any sentence that's chock-full of information and ask, "What did I just read?" Decide if you really understood it, or if you want to reread to make sure you caught it all.

**What it is** Speaking generally, fiction allows us to get "lost" or "transported," or to "fall into the world of the story"—the kind of reading experience that stirs what Louise Rosenblatt (1978) calls the "aesthetic response." Nonfiction, by contrast, demands we sit up and pay attention.

**How I'd teach it** For example, in *Sharks and Other Sea Creatures* (2000), Leighton Taylor writes, "Having a backbone, or a vertebral column, is what distinguishes our group of creatures—called vertebrates—from invertebrates, such as insects, spiders, and shellfishes, that have no backbones." This sentence is chock-full of information. Think aloud: "Hmm, Taylor is discussing how humans are part of the vertebrate group, meaning creatures that have backbones. So we're like sharks and whales. 'Distinguishes from' signals to me the author is setting up a contrast, so I know to read on for some kind of opposite. Yes: insects, spiders, and so on—no backbone. I can see how these invertebrate creatures are different from us vertebrates. Also, the author includes sharks but excludes other creatures like insects, spiders, and shellfish."

# Ask Questions, Read to Answer Them

**Strategy** Before reading a section, turn the heading or a first sentence into a question, or ask your own question about what you hope to learn in the section. As you read on, look for information that answers your question.

**What it is** Questioning is an important way to remain focused on and understand the purpose of a nonfiction text. Experienced nonfiction readers might pose a question unconsciously at the outset of a book, and then read on to get an answer. For example, one might ask: "I wonder why hurricanes occur most often in September?" Yet, for some, asking and answering these kinds of questions is an acquired habit, and these readers will benefit from modeling.

**How I'd teach it** Have students form questions inspired by headings and topic sentences. Books in the If You Lived When . . . series contain headings written as questions. Show students one of the books as a model and tell them that not all nonfiction books follow this format, but we can replicate it by turning headings and topic sentences into questions. Take Mary Atkinson's *Genius or Madman? Sir Isaac Newton* (2008). You could turn the heading "A Farming Failure" into the question, "Why was Sir Isaac Newton a failure at farming?" Then read on to find supporting details. You might use Seymour Simon's *Snakes* (2007), which contains the topic sentence, "Snakes can't walk or run, but they have at least three ways of moving." Turn this sentence into a question: "What are three ways that snakes move?" Students can then read for details with that question in mind.

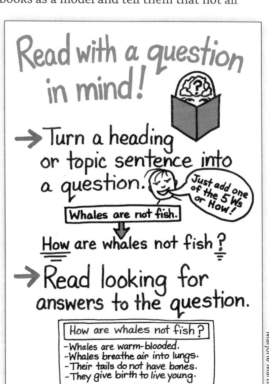

*Marjorie Martinelli*

## KD.3 — Stop, Scan, and Look

### Who is this for?

**LEVELS**

J–W

**SKILLS**

determining importance to support a main idea with key details from the text

**Strategy** Before turning a page, stop and scan to see if there is information in boxes and sidebars that supports the main idea. Then, look over photos, illustrations, and other visuals to pick up additional useful information.

**What it is** Help students remember they shouldn't just stick to the main text and pass off captions and sidebars as fluff and flourishes.

**How I'd teach it** For example, in *A Negro League Scrapbook* (2005) by Carole Weatherford, key details are contained in the captions. These support the idea that many of the baseball players were versatile.

Ted Radcliff was nicknamed "Double Duty" by writer Damon Runyon, who saw him play a doubleheader at Yankee Stadium. In the first game, Radcliff served as catcher for Satchel Paige. In the second game, he took the mound and pitched a shutout!

Martin Dihigo played every position on the field exceptionally well. He was inducted into the Hall of Fame in 1977.

Player/manager José Méndez won three straight National Negro League pennants with the Kansas City Monarchs between 1923 and 1925.

# Circle, Then Zoom In

**Strategy** Look first at all the features on a page, on a spread, or within a chapter or section. Think, "What are important facts I'm learning from these features?" Then go to the main text and think about how feature information relates to text.

**What it is** Offer students a way into reading that doesn't begin with the main text. Like a hawk circling a mouse on the ground, have students survey eye-catching photos and sidebars before zooming in. This strategy helps many readers engage, focus, and, when necessary, muster the courage to tackle dense text.

**How I'd teach it** Penelope Arlon and Tory Gordon-Harris' *Penguins* (2012) includes many text features on each page that point toward the main idea. The reader can study pictures of penguins in zoos or waddling to their breeding grounds with captions such as "The penguins are tagged so they can be studied throughout the year" and "Zoos often breed penguins. The keepers study them as they grow, which helps them understand how penguins behave. This is very useful knowledge when protecting them in the wild." These features alone, separate from the text, give readers enough information to learn certain concepts, such as humans studying penguins to find ways to help them survive.

*Who is this for?*

**LEVELS**
J–W

**SKILLS**
determining importance to support a main idea with key details from the text

Features First!
1. Look at all the text features.
2. Think, "What important facts am I learning?"
3. Read the text and ask, "How does the text help me learn more?"

Now I'm learning...

graph
heading
photograph
caption
diagram

Lauren Knoke

# KD.5

# Know It Enough to Teach It

Barbara Golub

## Who is this for?

**LEVELS**

J–W

**SKILLS**

determining importance to support a main idea with key details from the text

**Strategy** If you know you'll meet with a partner to teach them about what you've learned, be sure to prepare as you read. Have your main idea in mind, then read on, asking yourself, "What examples can I give of information that supports that idea?"

**What it is** Every couple of weeks, let students know they're going to present some aspect of the book they are reading to their partners. Partners could be classmates or "buddies" from a younger grade for whom your students would serve as teachers.

Another option is to set your classroom up as a "courtroom," with one student as the prosecutor who cross-examines another student, or witness, on a topic. The witness creates the questions they'll be asked and prepared to answer after reading the book by providing a main idea and key details. Questions need to lend themselves to more than just a simple answer, and invite elaboration, for example, "What happened once it was clear that the *Titanic* was sinking? Why are dolphins smart, and why should they be used by the U.S. Navy? How do you know global warming is real?" and so forth.

**How I'd teach it** If a student is reading Peter Benoit's *September 11: We Will Never Forget* (2012), they might choose this idea: there was a lot of destruction on September 11th. These are some details that a student might give: "Nearly 3,000 people, from more than 90 countries, died on September 11th," or "Heat and smoke made escape almost impossible for the people located above the points where the jets hit." The student might also choose to prepare pictures in advance to support this information. What is key here is that students thread the details together under the umbrella of a larger main idea.

DO YOU KNOW IT ENOUGH TO TEACH IT?

1. Read about your topic

2. Name the main idea

3. Get specific with examples

4. Can you teach it to your partner?
YOU    PARTNER

# What's Important in the String of Events?

**Strategy**  When reading nonfiction in which the whole text or part of the text is written in a narrative structure, it's helpful to understand that the important details often come in the form of events. Think first, "What point is the author trying to make by choosing to tell this particular story?" and then, "Which events best make that point?"

**What it is**  Readers need to shift the way they collect key information when the text shifts from expository to narrative. This strategy will help a reader distinguish essential information from less crucial information inside of true stories they find in their information texts.

**How I'd teach it**  When reading *Koko's Kitten* by Francine Patterson (1985), a moving account of a gorilla who must deal with grief when her kitten dies, you might wonder aloud, "What's the author's point in giving an account of this story? Well, I think the author is trying to teach readers that gorillas are capable of communicating their feelings and emotions. Now, let me think about which events best support that point. There's the fact that Koko was able to learn sign language. She learned about 500 words. Also, Koko felt strong emotions throughout the book, for instance, when she was angry that she didn't get a kitten as a present and then felt depressed when she learned of Ball's death."

## KD.7 Recognize Trivia

**LEVELS**

J–W

**SKILLS**

determining importance to support a main idea with key details from the text

**Strategy** Determine the difference between facts that enhance key understanding and ones that are just plain fun. Keep this thought in mind as you read: "Does this fact fit with the heading or main idea of this section?" If the answer is no, you should tuck the fact away, knowing it's not key to supporting the main idea.

**What it is** Authors sometimes include trivial information that is meant to shock, startle, or entertain the reader more than help them understand the main idea(s) of the book. Sometimes these factoids are found in boxes or sidebars, and sometimes in the main text.

**How I'd teach it** For example, in the book *You Wouldn't Want to Be a Nurse During the American Civil War!* by Kathryn Senior (2010), the spread on pages 18–19 is about how surgery on the field was often dangerous. Callouts such as the following provide tangential information that keeps the reader engaged, but does not directly support the main idea: "After the war, soldiers with amputated limbs have a hard time finding work. Many have to beg for food and money," and "Better not be squeamish. As a Civil War nurse, you're going to see a whole lot of blood." Therefore, the information in these captions could be considered trivial when assessing key details that support a main idea.

70

# Do You Know or Do You Think You Know?

**Strategy** When you come upon a fact that contradicts something you think you know and find yourself saying, "Hmm. This is different from what I thought," ask yourself, "What is the information the author is teaching? What information fits the main idea of this page?"

**What it is** To get readers to engage and interact with nonfiction texts, it's important to activate prior knowledge. However, if a reader's prior knowledge is inaccurate, activating it can actually hurt more than help. So it's important to teach readers, as they approach a text, to compare their perceived knowledge about the topic to the information the author actually presents.

**How I'd teach it** You could use an article like "Thanksgiving: Myth and Fact" (2001) in a small group or conference to show students that often we come to a topic with ideas that turn out to be misconceptions. As readers, it is important to check our prior knowledge against the information presented in a text to make sure we understand what the author is setting out to teach, and what information fits that main idea.

> DO YOU KNOW? OR DO YOU THINK YOU KNOW?
>
> 1. READ!
> 2. Pay attention to FACTS that CHALLENGE what you think you know.
> 3. THINK!
>    - "Hm. This is different from what I thought." AND
>    - "What information fits the main idea of this page?" AND
>    - "What information is the author teaching?"

Barbara Golub

# KD.9

# Find Patterns

## Who is this for?

**LEVELS**

J–W

**SKILLS**

determining
importance to
support a main
idea with key
details from
the text

**Strategy** Look for words that repeat—the same word or a synonym of that word.
Add up the facts associated with the repeating words. Then think, "What do all of
these facts have in common?"

**What it is** The most important information in a text often reiterates, supports,
or proves the author's main point. In some texts, the author will repeat a key word
or use synonyms for that word from one sentence to the next to make their point
inarguably clear.

**How I'd teach it** In *How to Clean a Hippopotamus* by Steve Jenkins and Robin
Page (2010), the word *symbiosis* appears throughout.

- "These creatures—and many others—have formed relationships in which each
  animal helps the other. This is called symbiosis."

- "The sea anemone and the clownfish, with its immunity to the anemone's
  poisonous tentacles, are one of the best-known examples of animal symbiosis."

- "Dogs and humans have lived together for thousands of years. Their relationship
  is probably the most commonly observed symbiosis in the animal world."

- "We've looked
  at just a few of
  the mutualistic
  symbiotic
  relationships
  in the animal
  world."

The reader can
conclude that these
details support the
idea of a give-and-
take relationship
among animals.

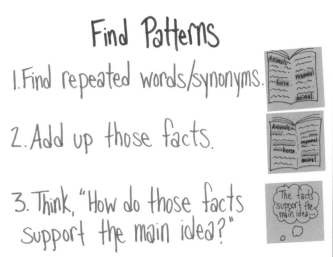

Find Patterns

1. Find repeated words/synonyms.

2. Add up those facts.

3. Think, "How do those facts support the main idea?"

Lauren Knoke

# Strongly Worded Facts

**Strategy** Think about the slant the author has on the topic. Look out for facts that contain words that relate back to the main idea. Reread these facts thinking, "How does this support the main idea?"

**What it is** If you can determine the author's slant on a topic, you can look for facts that support it. For example, if the author writes early on that sharks are scary, you can look for words that relate to hunting prey: *fierce*, *hunting grounds*, and *razor-sharp teeth*. Facts that contain words with similar meanings are likely to relate back to the main idea. By contrast, readers wouldn't find support for the main idea by looking at, say, sidebars on the shark-skin industry or some cultures' medicinal use of sharks.

**How I'd teach it** In *Oh, Rats!* (2006), Albert Marrin expresses an opinion in the topic sentence: "Everything about the rat makes it a champion at survival" (10). Phrases such as *keen senses*, *excellent night vision*, and *marvelous sense of balance* back up the author's notion. You can think aloud for students about how you notice the connection between all the terms. All of these details give the reader insight into the author's point of view. The author clearly thinks rats have amazing qualities that make them really sturdy creatures that are adept at survival.

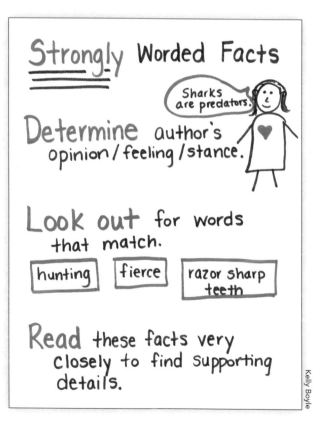

Kelly Boyle

## Who is this for?

**LEVELS**
J–W

**SKILLS**

determining importance to support a main idea with key details from the text

# KD.11 Lean on the Problem and Solution

**LEVELS**

J–W

**SKILLS**

determining importance to support a main idea with key details from the text

**Strategy** When reading biography, notice places where the historical figure faces obstacles or challenges. Then pay attention to how they persevere despite those challenges. Name what you learn about the person based on their actions.

**What it is** In narrative nonfiction, just as in fictional narratives, the problem and the solution to that problem are key to understanding important information. Teach readers to lean on what they know from reading fiction to help them read narrative nonfiction.

**How I'd teach it** For example, in *Wolfgang Amadeus Mozart* by Mike Venezia (1995), page 18 reads, "Another problem was that Wolfgang and Nannerl were growing up. People didn't find them quite as cute and remarkable as they once had. Wolfgang knew he would have to amaze people now by writing and playing the best music ever—which is just what he did." Here, the reader can first identify the challenge: Wolfgang was growing up and people didn't find him quite as endearing as they once had. Then they can analyze how Wolfgang dealt with this problem: he continued to work hard despite the challenges he faced. Finally, the reader can ask the question, "What is this teaching me about Wolfgang?" and answer it: "Wolfgang was not the type of person who easily gives up."

74

# Use the Pictures to Support You

**Strategy**  Look closely at the text features and images within the section. Look for details within each feature, and compare what you learn. Think, "What similar information do you learn from two images or features? What information is different?"

**What it is**  To make rich comparisons, readers need to look not only in the main text, but also in the pictures and other text features. For some readers, doing that before delving into the main text may help them comprehend the whole text more deeply.

**How I'd teach it**  In *Surprising Sharks*, Nicola Davies (2003) writes, "In fact, sharks come in all sorts of shapes and sizes" (13). The picture on that page illustrates this by showing a range of sharks—an angel shark, a cookie-cutter shark, and a goblin shark— that are all different shapes and sizes. Here, the pictures provide the supporting details, and readers can use them to compare and contrast different sharks.

**Tip**  This strategy is likely to be most helpful in texts where the page layout is more straightforward—usually just a picture and corresponding text. When the pages get busier, there is an added challenge in navigating those pages.

## Who is this for?

**LEVELS**

J–W

**SKILLS**

comparing and contrasting key details

# KD.13

# Go Outside the Book

**LEVELS**

J–W

**SKILLS**

comparing and contrasting key details

**Strategy** Find and read two books on the same topic. Think, "What information is consistent between the two books? What information does one author give that the other doesn't? Is there any information that one author provides that the other author would disagree with?"

**What it is** Students can practice their ability to compare and contrast information when they look for comparisons not only within the same text, but also between multiple texts.

**How I'd teach it** You can organize your classroom library to encourage this comparison. Find books that fit together and bundle them with rubber bands or inside zip-top plastic bags. The narrower the topic, the easier it'll be for a child to read across that topic. For example, a bag about sharks—with books on great white sharks and whale sharks—will set a child up for easier comparisons than a bag about ocean animals—with books on topics ranging from seahorses to whales. Creating book bags about anything from athletes to artists to different forms of government will help students. Then you can encourage children to read across the books using any of the strategies described in this section.

# Speak the Language of Comparison

**Strategy**  When comparing two topics, think first about whether the two pieces of information show what's the same or what's different. Then, choose a language frame to help you talk about the two. Compare = same, contrast = different.

**What it is**  It's one thing for students to notice when two parts of a text can be compared. It's another thing for them to have the language to actually make the comparison. Sentence starters and language frames can offer helpful scaffolding to support students as they work to articulate comparisons.

**How I'd teach it**  When coaching children during book clubs, partnerships, or whole-class conversations, I'd offer them language that would help prompt them to compare and/or contrast. Following are some examples of the language you might teach:

- (contrast) In this section, I learned _____, but in this section it says _____.

- (compare) Two things that are similar about _____ and _____ are _____.

- (compare) One thing that's alike between _____ and _____ is _____. But something that is different is _____.

- (contrast) With _____, I understand that _____. However, with _____ it's actually _____.

- (compare) Just like with _____, I learned that also _____.

## Who is this for?

**LEVELS**

J–W

**SKILLS**

comparing and contrasting key details

DARE TO COMPARE!

Use these tips to help you talk!

In this section, I learned ——, but in this section it says ——.

Two things that are similar between — and — are —— and ——. Something that is different is ——.

With ——, I understand that ——, however with —— it's actually ——

Kristine Mraz

## KD.15 — Use Superlatives

### Who is this for?

**LEVELS**

J–W

**SKILLS**

comparing and
contrasting
key details

**Strategy** Look for the author's use of superlatives in the headings or facts. Think, "In what way do I expect to see the information being compared, or ranked?" If the author doesn't use superlatives but seems to be ranking a range of similar topics, you can create your own heading using a superlative.

**What it is** Sometimes organizing information by ranking things will help students make comparisons. Using superlatives such as *greatest*, *meanest*, *fastest*, *strongest*, *tallest*, *shortest*, and so on, can be a starting place for comparisons.

**How I'd teach it** Steve Jenkins and Robin Page include superlatives in several headings in their book *Animals in Flight* (2001). You could have students turn to the heading "The Largest and Smallest Flyers," and help them understand how it sets the reader up to compare and contrast the flying animals discussed on pages 23 and 24.

Students can also read information and use comparatives to arrive at their own rankings: <u>this fish</u> *is faster than* <u>this fish</u> because of the size of its tail, or <u>the giraffe</u> *is taller than* <u>the elephant</u> because it needs to use its long neck to reach the upper branches of a tree.

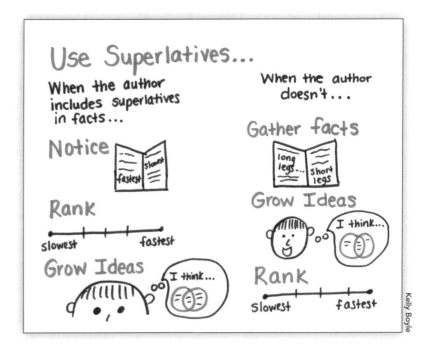

# Think in Categories

**Strategy** For each topic, make a list of the categories: parts, kinds, or reasons. Then think about the details you learn about each related to those parts, kinds, or reasons and ask yourself, "What does the author tell me about what's the same? What does the author tell me about what's different?" When comparing the two topics, organize the facts based on categories.

**What it is** Students who focus heavily on the main idea may have a hard time comparing details. Those students think "big picture," and when asked to support that picture with specifics from the text, they may just shrug. So when you ask them to zoom in on details, teach them to rely on their strengths and think in categories: parts, kinds, or reasons. When the information in the text isn't already organized into part, kind, or reason categories, readers can reorganize information into their own categories to compare what they've learned.

**How I'd teach it** When comparing two animals (say, a snake and a lizard), readers can ask themselves, "What are the *parts* of these two animals?" They can list: skin, tongue, eyes, teeth, and so on. Then they can think, "What does the author tell me about each of these animal parts in the text and the pictures that lets me know some things are alike about the animals? What is something the author tells me about the parts that lets me know the animals are different?"

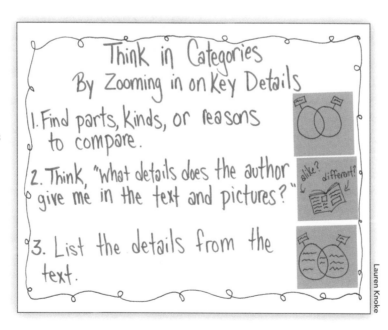

Think in Categories
By Zooming in on Key Details

1. Find parts, kinds, or reasons to compare.

2. Think, "what details does the author give me in the text and pictures?"

3. List the details from the text.

Lauren Knoke

# KD.17 Identify a Compare-and-Contrast Structure

## Who is this for?

**LEVELS**

O–W

**SKILLS**

comparing and contrasting

key details

**Strategy** Look out for words and phrases that show an author is comparing or contrasting: *unlike, by contrast, on the other hand, while, yet, but, rather, either, like/ unlike, some, as opposed to, as well as, compared to/compared with, on the other hand, although, the same, similarly*. Notice the information that comes before and after these key words and phrases, think, "How is this information related?"

**What it is** Sometimes texts are set up with an inherently compare-and-contrast structure. To help students identify a compare and/or contrast structure while reading, you can often encourage them to look for transition words and phrases.

**How I'd teach it** To demonstrate the strategy, I might display this sentence from Fiona Macdonald's *You Wouldn't Want to Be a Medieval Knight!* (2004) using a document camera, and read it aloud: "Compared with knights, most foot soldiers are only part-time fighters, but this does not make them any less dangerous" (25). From there, I might say, "*Compared with*—that means two things are being put side by side. (The author is saying that unlike knights, foot soldiers fight only part-time.) Then the word *but* appears, signaling a change in the comparison. (Even with this difference, there's a similarity: like knights, foot soldiers are dangerous.)"

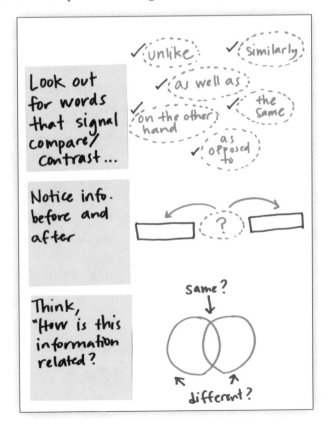

# Use a Venn Diagram or Three-Column Chart

**Strategy** After reading a fact, pause and ask yourself, "Where does this information fit? Is it something that's the same as or similar to something else that was described, or is it different?" Place the information where it belongs on the chart or Venn diagram so it's organized when you review it.

**What it is** Graphic organizers can be helpful tools for visually sorting information that's presented in a text. A Venn diagram is a simple organizer made up of two or more overlapping circles in which similar items are placed in the overlapping portion, while dissimilar items are placed in the nonoverlapping portions. A three-column chart can function like a Venn diagram if similar information is placed in the middle column, while dissimilar information is placed in the outer columns.

**How I'd teach it** Take the book *Hungry Plants* by Mary Batten (2000). Each chapter discusses a different carnivorous plant. Readers can identify what is similar and different about those types of plants, and then capture their findings in a Venn diagram or three-column chart.

**Tip** Keep in mind that graphic organizers are just that—organizers. So in addition to the organizer, be sure to give students a strategy to help them know how to sort through the information in their book and transfer it to the organizer.

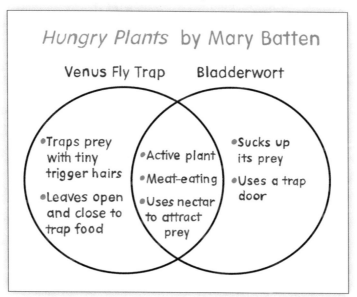

*Hungry Plants* by Mary Batten

Venus Fly Trap        Bladderwort

- Traps prey with tiny trigger hairs
- Leaves open and close to trap food

- Active plant
- Meat-eating
- Uses nectar to attract prey

- Sucks up its prey
- Uses a trap door

## Who is this for?

**LEVELS**

O–W

**SKILLS**

comparing and contrasting key details

## KD.19 — Compare Apples to Apples

### Who is this for?

**LEVELS**

O–W

**SKILLS**

comparing and contrasting key details

**Strategy**  Think about two topics you're reading about that are similar in some way. Compare the details about each by thinking, "Within each category, what's the same and what's different?"

**What it is**  Nonfiction texts often contain signal words, such as *however*, *although*, and *but*, to suggest that two things are being compared. Sometimes, however, they don't. Thinking in categories helps a reader to know when the author is comparing two related concepts, people, or things. For example, a book about space travel is more likely to compare two astronauts than it is to compare an astronaut and a spaceship. Teach students to compare the same types of things.

**How I'd teach it**  Books about rivalries work really well for teaching this strategy. Throughout history, famous people have often tried to outdo rivals with the same goal, from baseball players bent on hitting the most home runs to scientists trying to cure diseases. So there are many options when it comes to choosing texts that work well when you are teaching readers to be on the lookout for rivalries that highlight a subject's essential character traits and contributions. Whatever text you choose, keep modeling for students how to think about the parts of each topic they read about, and to compare within categories for each topic.

COMPARE LIKE THINGS

1. READ!

2. Be on the lookout for **RIVALRIES**

3. ASK:

- "Are there things about these people/concepts/objects that are alike?"

- "Are there things about these people/concepts/objects that are different?"

Barbara Golub

# How Do These Parts Connect?

**Strategy** As you move from one section of a text to another, it's helpful to consider how the information in each section connects. Compare key details between sections by thinking, "What's the same about the information in this part and that part? What's different?"

**What it is** Authors sometimes juxtapose facts to encourage the reader to make comparisons and connections across sections in a text.

**How I'd teach it** The article "Celebrate Hispanic Heritage!" (2007) is subtitled "Many Hispanic Americans Have Made Important Contributions in Their Chosen Field." Each section talks about a different famous person: Roberto Clemente, Antonia Novello, Gloria Estefan. A reader is set up to ask, "How is each person's contribution similar, and how is each person's contribution different?"

In the article "Coming to America" (2003), the first two sections are "Ellis Island" and "Angel Island: The Ellis Island of the West Coast." When reading these two sections side by side, a reader should be able to list key details about both places, and then compare what makes them similar and what makes them different.

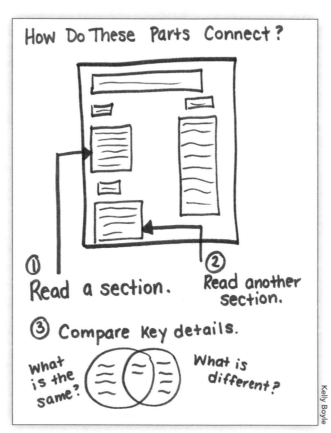

## Who is this for?

**LEVELS**

O–W

**SKILLS**

comparing and contrasting key details

## KD.21  Compare Perspectives

**LEVELS**

O–W

**SKILLS**

comparing and
contrasting
key details

**Strategy**  Think: "What in a person's background might make them view the event in this way? What do they have to gain or lose? What are all the impacts of this event? How does this person's perspective compare with the author's or another person's perspective?"

**What it is**  People with different stakes in an event, or with different backgrounds, may experience an event very differently. When the author writes about the same event or experience more than once within the same text, it's likely that a new perspective is being offered.

**How I'd teach it**  There are times when different perspectives will appear in a sidebar—as in Sandra Newman's *Ancient Greece* (2010); at other times they will be embedded within the text—as in Russell Freedman's *Immigrant Kids* (1980); and sometimes you may see them in their own sections. In a lesson, it can be helpful to show children these different ways that they may come upon varying perspectives so that they can be on the lookout for them in their own books, too.

---

### Perspective: It Matters

⭐ People can experience the same event differently:
- Their stake in it matters
- Their background matters

⭐ So, consider:
- What in a person's background might make them view the event this way?
- What does s/he have to gain? Lose?
- What are each of the impacts of the event?
- How does this person's perspective compare with the author's? Another person's?

Barbara Golub

# Identifying Multiple Perspectives

**Strategy** As you read, think about whose voice is heard and whose is not. Consider whose perspective is represented, and what groups may have been left out. Notice who you hear more from, and what that makes you wonder.

**What it is** To compare information, it's helpful to have a sense of the different perspectives presented in the text.

**How I'd teach it** In *Endangered Animals* (1984), Lynn Stone writes, "Not all countries have tough laws. A hunter in Africa may sneak into a national park. He kills a leopard. He is breaking the law, but the park is big. He is hard to catch. He knows he can sell the leopard's fur. Perhaps he cannot sell the fur in Africa, but people in another country will buy the fur for a high price. You see, unless all countries stop selling endangered animal parts, the animal will always be in danger" (32). You can think aloud for students about this section, "The perspective represented is likely that of endangered animals and conservationists. Whose perspective is not represented here? Well, the poachers' perspective and the perspective of leopard-skin traders, and people who purchase the fur. What we don't read about are the participants: their living conditions and economic status and what causes them to involve themselves in the killing and selling of animals and animal parts."

*Who is this for?*

**LEVELS**
O–W

**SKILLS**

comparing and contrasting key details

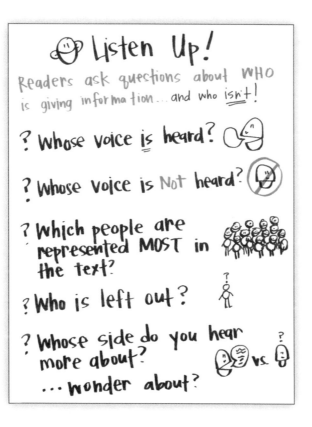

😊 Listen Up!

Readers ask questions about WHO is giving information... and who isn't!

? Whose voice is heard?

? Whose voice is Not heard?

? Which people are represented MOST in the text?

? Who is left out?

? Whose side do you hear more about?
... wonder about?

## KD.23 — Compare Past and Present

**LEVELS**

O-W

**SKILLS**

comparing and
contrasting
key details

**Strategy** Think about an event in history or present day that connects to an event that you're reading about. Compare the people, issue, or concept across time periods.

**What it is** When students are learning about history, it's likely that an author will help them understand how events connect across time. It's important for readers to compare time periods, especially when they share a uniting feature.

**How I'd teach it** When teaching about the Civil Rights Movement in the 1960s, help students think back to the period of slavery in America and how some of the struggles of African Americans in the 1960s have their roots in how Africans were treated in America earlier in history. It's also helpful to think ahead to the present day, and the civil rights issues still facing African Americans, or other marginalized groups such as LGBTQ Americans, or Hispanic immigrants. Teaching students to take notes from their books using a timeline or other graphic organizer may be one way for them to look across points in history to draw comparisons or articulate contrasting events, viewpoints, and perspectives.

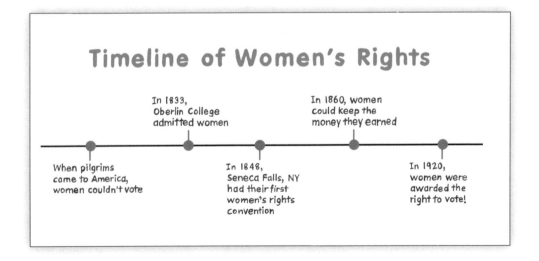

### Timeline of Women's Rights

In 1833, Oberlin College admitted women

In 1860, women could keep the money they earned

When pilgrims came to America, women couldn't vote

In 1848, Seneca Falls, NY had their first women's rights convention

In 1920, women were awarded the right to vote!

# Compare Historical Figures and Their Perspectives

**Strategy** When you read about real people in your nonfiction book, you can think, "What kind of person is he or she? (Nice? Moody? Selfish? Giving? Popular? Trustworthy? And so on.) How must they have felt? What might they have thought about these important events?" Then compare that one person's experience with that of another person who was alive at the same time and experienced the same event.

**What it is** Help students apply their knowledge of fictional characters and character change to think more deeply about historical figures.

**How I'd teach it** In Kenneth Davis' *Don't Know Much About the Presidents* (2001), a student will learn: "When George Washington was elected America's first president, John Adams was elected the first vice president. The vice president's main job is to fill in if anything happens to the president. But Adams wanted to be number one. So when Washington refused a third term, Adams ran for president himself" (11). A reader could ask, "What kind of person was he?" and say, "Adams was ambitious. He wanted to be a leader." And then ask, "How must he have felt when he won?" and say, "He must have felt like he finally got what he wanted." The reader could compare Adams to Washington, looking at passages that focus on Washington: "His countrymen believed in him. They wanted him to lead the new nation because he'd been the heroic general of the Continental Army" (29) and "People liked George Washington so much that some wanted to crown him king" (46). Then the reader might infer that Washington was humbler than Adams, or that he stepped into the presidency at the urging of the people, while Adams really took the initiative to put himself there.

## Who is this for?

**LEVELS**
O–W

**SKILLS**
comparing and contrasting key details

Historical Figures are Characters!

1. Think, "What kind of person is he or she?" *hardworking? caring? selfish? trustworthy?*

2. Ask, "How might he/she have felt or thought about important events?"

3. Compare two historical figures or their two perspectives. *What happened? Ideas about the people?*

Lauren Knoke

Monitoring for
meaning and using
context

# Vocabulary

Understanding a text's vocabulary has been empirically linked to reading comprehension, which is why it deserves a prominent place in this assessment and teaching resource (Baumann and Kame'enui 1991; Beck, McKeown, and Kucan 2013; Becker 1977; Stanovich 1986). Research shows that if students are truly to understand what they read, they must grasp upward of 95 percent of the words they encounter (Betts 1946; Carver 1994; Hu and Nation 2000; Laufer 1988).

Interestingly, research has also shown that although it is helpful to explicitly teach words and phrases to readers, most word learning occurs unconsciously, in the acts of reading, writing, speaking, and listening (Baumann, Kame'enui, and Ash 2003; Krashen 2004; Miller 1999; Nagy, Anderson, and Herman 1987).

# Monitoring for Meaning and Using Context

As you begin to use the results from the assessment to teach vocabulary, keep in mind that as texts become more challenging, so do the words. Moreover, the frequency of challenging words increases. Up to Level M, a reader needs to use simple context to give an accurate definition of a word—usually just the sentence in which the word appears and/or a photo or illustration that somehow visually captures the word. Beginning at Level M, however, a reader needs to use more than immediate context and text features beyond photos and illustrations. They also need to do more than define the word—and instead need to explain or describe it. In other words, the reader must demonstrate an understanding, not simply parrot back a definition provided by the author. Beginning at Level O, a reader must demonstrate a deep understanding of the word by relating it to their understanding of the page or section.

# Strategies for Understanding Vocabulary at a Glance

# Strategies for Understanding Vocabulary at a Glance

# V.1

# Show Off Your Expertise

**LEVELS**
J–W

**SKILLS**

monitoring for meaning and using context

**Strategy**  Keep notes of interesting vocabulary and concepts as you read. Be in the habit of asking yourself, "Have I used the most precise words I can?" Go back to the text and find words that will help you teach about your topic.

**What it is**  Students often go the extra mile to learn content-specific vocabulary and concepts when they know they are going to have to present to a peer. Create situations in which students have to share their nonfiction knowledge—with the class, a partner, or a buddy in a lower grade.

**How I'd teach it**  For example, if you are conferring with a student as they are reading Laura Layton Strom's *The Egyptian Science Gazette: Where the News Is Ancient History* (2007), encourage the reader to use words such as *pharaoh*, *tomb*, *sarcophagus*, and *hieroglyphics*. Students can collect subject-specific words in their reading notebooks and call on these terms during their partner talk and writing about reading.

# Use Glossaries

**Strategy** Pause when you come to a word that is highlighted (bold, italics, in color). Look for where that word may be defined (glossary, sidebar). Read the definition. Go back to the context where the word appears and insert the definition or a synonym back into the sentence. Explain what the word means.

**What it is** When authors use content words, they often define those words explicitly in the margin or in a glossary at the back of the book. They also may highlight the words in some way—with bold print, color, or italics. It's important for students to take the time to read the definition rather than breeze by it. In the end, they should be able to explain what the word means in the context of the book they are reading.

**How I'd teach it** In *Pandemics* (2012), Kevin Cunningham writes, "Poor sanitation in 19th-century cities aided its [cholera's] spread by providing the bacterium a place to flourish" (16). If the reader looks up the word *sanitation* in the glossary, they will find: "The process of making things clean and healthy." This will give them a fuller understanding of the word and an awareness that it doesn't pertain to cholera outbreaks of the 1800s only. Knowing a word deeply and being able to apply it in many contexts (in subsequent reading, writing, and conversations) create a snowball effect by helping students unlock word meanings with ever-growing acuity.

**Who is this for?**

LEVELS
J–W

SKILLS
monitoring for meaning and using context

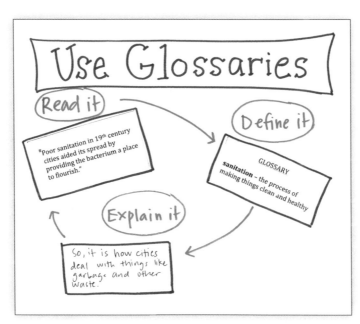

## V.3

# Lean on Text Features

*Who is this for?*

**LEVELS**

J–W

**SKILLS**

monitoring for
meaning
and using
context

**Strategy** Often words that relate to a key concept are supported by a photograph or illustration. Study its details. Think, "What in this image relates to the word I'm trying to learn?" Take what you notice and use it to explain the meaning of the word.

**What it is** Nonfiction for children often includes engaging text features such as photos and captions, illustrations, maps, and boxes. These features can help a reader to learn details and to understand vocabulary.

**How I'd teach it** In Robert D. Ballard's *Exploring the Titanic* (1989), a section begins, "The morning of July 18 was lovely and warm, but I felt edgy about the day's mission. We had decided to visit the Titanic's debris field" (52). If a reader doesn't know the word *debris*, it could interfere with their comprehension of the section. But by studying the picture collage on that page, the reader can deduce the word's meaning. Model this by thinking aloud: "Ah, *debris* must mean 'wreckage.' The field around the Titanic is strewn with ship parts, china and glass, and the passengers' items."

Barbara Golub

# Insert a Somewhat-Synonym

**Strategy** When you come to a new content-specific word, think about the information you're learning. In place of the new word, insert a word you know that is close to the meaning of the word in the text.

**What it is** Although it's important for readers to learn the language of experts when reading a nonfiction text, determining the meaning of vocabulary should not slow down the reading too much or feel like a chore. When students persevere for too long in trying to understand a word's meaning, they may become discouraged or lose sight of the overall meaning of the section. At times, it's appropriate for a reader to substitute a word that makes sense in the context of the sentence, even if they know it might not be a precise synonym. In this way, the reader will still leave with an overall gist or basic understanding of that section as well as of the word.

**How I'd teach it** As you read aloud to students and come upon a content-specific word that may be new to you, model thinking aloud: "Hmm. I don't know this word. But if I think about what I'm learning here, I could stick in a synonym. I think in this case, *habitat* might mean 'home.' Let me stick in the word *home* for *habitat* and see if that makes sense."

## Who is this for?

**LEVELS**

J–W

**SKILLS**

monitoring for meaning and using context

Unsure what a word means?
Insert a Somewhat-Synonym!

1. Pause when you come to a new content-specific word.

2. Substitute a word that makes sense in the context of the sentence.

Lauren Knoke

# V.5 Tricks for Spotting Clues in Context

**LEVELS**

J–W

**SKILLS**

monitoring for meaning and using context

**Strategy** Look for a definition of the word right in the text. Read the couple of sentences *before* the word, read the sentence *in which the word appears*, and *read on* for a couple of sentences. Be on the lookout for the word to be repeated, or for commas or parentheses with a definition tucked inside (i.e., "_____ means" or "_____ is").

**What it is** Students don't always know what it means to use context clues, so it's crucial to model how you do that. Show them precise places and ways to look for clues.

**How I'd teach it** Writers of nonfiction texts up to Level O will often define a word in a nearby sentence. Consider these lines from Avelyn Davidson's *A Day in the Life of an African Village* (2008): "However, deforestation is threatening the Ituri forests. Timber and mining companies are cutting down thousands of trees" (18).

Another common way in which authors define words is to offer a synonym in a parenthetical clause within the sentence. Or they might set it apart with commas or dashes. Consider this sentence from Steven Jenkins' *Bones* (2010): "Animals . . . have a spine, or backbone, made of bones called vertebrae" (20).

At other times, the definition will come in a sentence before or after the word, as in this example from Molly Aloian and Bobbie Kalman's *Endangered Frogs* (2006): "Every animal goes through a set of changes from the time it is born or hatches from an egg to the time it is an adult. This set of changes is called a life cycle" (8).

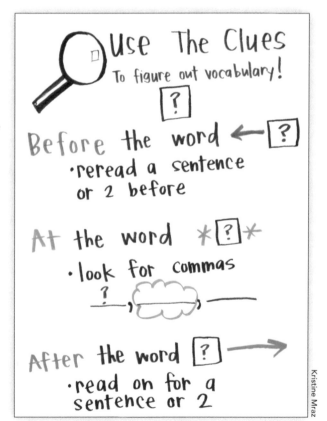

Kristine Mraz

# Say It

**Strategy**  When you find a word you don't recognize, work to read it carefully. Use any of your decoding strategies (reading part by part, covering and sliding over the word, trying different vowel sounds, etc.). Listen as you read it and think, "Have I heard that word before, even if I haven't seen it written?"

**What it is**  Model how you play around with the word by voicing the sounds the letters in the word could make until students arrive at the correct pronunciation. As they do, the more likely they are to have an aha! moment of word recognition. This is a helpful strategy for a reader who has a strong speaking vocabulary yet seems to have difficulty when encountering new words in texts.

**How I'd teach it**  As you model this strategy, be sure to show students how placing the emphasis on different syllables in the word can make the word one they recognize or, in some cases, can change the word's meaning. For example, you may break up the word *hibernation* into syllables, emphasizing the first syllable (HI-bernation), then the third syllable (hi-ber-NA-tion). Think aloud as you apply other strategies, such as trying different sounds each vowel can make.

*Merridy Gnagey*

### Who is this for?

**LEVELS**
J–W

**SKILLS**
monitoring for meaning and using context

# V.7 Use It or Lose It

**LEVELS**

J–W

**SKILLS**

monitoring for meaning and using context

**Strategy** Make a word bank for yourself with the words you find and learn. Include synonyms, antonyms, and a context sentence to help you remember what the word means. Keep the word bank nearby when discussing or writing about your learning.

**What it is** Even when the text makes the meaning of new vocabulary clear by giving context or text-feature support, children need multiple exposures to a word before making it part of their permanent vocabulary. People need repeated experience with a new word to learn it—they need to hear or read the word; they need to understand what the word is (its synonyms) and what it is not (its antonyms); and they need to put the word into a meaningful context, using it in their own speech or writing. Technical vocabulary especially, with its infrequent real-world usage, unconventional spellings, and perhaps difficult pronunciation, is not the easiest or most natural for children to incorporate into their own language.

**How I'd teach it** If you are reading aloud Laura Layton Strom's *Caught with a Catch: Poaching in Africa* (2008b), you might pause after reading a defining sentence such as, "Also, the sale of animal parts is a lucrative way for soldiers to get money for weapons" (14). Take the word *lucrative* and write it in the middle of a chart. List a few synonyms (*profitable, well paid, rewarding*) and an antonym or two (*unprofitable, poorly paid*). Write a sentence to use the word, such as "Selling animal parts is a lucrative business. It makes hunters seven billion dollars each year." Finally, have students include it in their writing about reading, or in their talk with their partner.

Kristine Mraz

# Become an Actor

**Strategy**  Stop when you come to a confusing word or part. Act out what's being described. Think, "What's this part really about? So, what might this word mean?"

**What it is**  Encourage students to move their bodies and/or gesture if they feel stuck in the quicksand of a difficult word or text.

**How I'd teach it**  As students act out what's being described in the text, the meanings of any unknown words may reveal themselves. Physically representing the words on the page aids visualization, and visualizing the text will help the reader to understand context. For example, in Martin Jenkins' *Chameleons Are Cool* (2001), the topic sentence on page 22 reads, "Now, peering about is something chameleons are good at." If readers are unable to get the word *peering*, they should read on, acting out the information that follows: "That's because their eyes can move separately from each other, unlike our eyes, which always move together." (Kids might practice moving each eye here.) "So while one eye is looking back over the chameleon's shoulder, the other one is scanning the branches ahead." (Kids can try this out!) Now students can go back and see if they can figure out what the word *peering* means, thinking about what body part they were mostly using as they acted out the text, and any patterns in their movements.

Kelly Boyle

**LEVELS**
J–W

**SKILLS**

monitoring for meaning and using context

# V.9  Keep a Tally

## Who is this for?

**LEVELS**

J–W

**SKILLS**

monitoring for meaning and using context

**Strategy**  Keep track of words you learn while reading that you want to know and use. Keep a tally each time you read the word, say the word, and use the word in your writing.

**What it is**  Research shows that for students to learn a new word, they need to hear the word, assign it their own context, and then use it multiple times in meaningful ways.

**How I'd teach it**  In your classroom, you might set up a bulletin board titled "Words We Use!" When students come upon new words they will try to use, they can put each on an index card with the definition below it. The class may also decide to add words from the read-aloud story to this chart. Each time a student uses a word, the user's name can be added to the card. Students can, of course, also keep their own personal cards on their desks and challenge themselves or their partner to use those words. Each use gets a tally mark.

Tiffany

{Go Words!}

| Words *I am learning | Read it | Said it | Wrote it |
|---|---|---|---|
| 1. contrary | I | IIII | II |
| 2. peer | III | IIII | III |
| 3. fervent | I | II | |
| 4. sensible | IIII | IIIII | I |

# Look Out for Key Words: Compare

**Strategy** Be on the lookout for words commonly used with comparisons, such as *and*, *or*, *same*, or *similarly*. Identify what two things are being compared. Then think, "Given what this part is teaching, what could the word mean?"

**What it is** A sentence might be structured by comparing two like things. In this case, readers need to be on the lookout for words that signal a comparison.

**How I'd teach it** Consider this sentence from Christine Puleo's "A Lifesaving Hug" (2000): "It dislodges, or removes, food that gets stuck in the throat and blocks breathing and speaking." Here, noticing *or* will help the reader understand that the words that come before and after it are synonyms.

*Who is this for?*

**LEVELS**

J–W

**SKILLS**

monitoring for meaning and using context

# V.11

# Look Out for Key Words: Contrast

## Who is this for?

**LEVELS**

J–W

**SKILLS**

monitoring for meaning and using context

**Strategy** Be on the lookout for words commonly used with contrasting two ideas or facts within a text, such as *while*, *but*, *not*, or *unlike*. Identify what two things are being contrasted. Then think, "Given what this part is teaching, what could the word mean?"

**What it is** Authors might try to set up the sentence to contrast or show two different things. Understanding the relationship between facts can help readers uncover the meaning of words.

**How I'd teach it** Take the following sentences from Michelle Markel's *Brave Girl: Clara and the Shirtwaist Makers' Strike of 1909* (2013): "For weeks the small strikes go on. But the bosses find other young women to do the work for the same low pay and long hours." Here, if the reader is unclear of the meaning of *strike*, they can use the structure of these two sentences to figure it out. The word *but* denotes a shift. Looking at the word *but* helps the reader understand that the word *strike* is in conflict with *work*. This tells the reader that *strike* could mean "refused" or "opposed" work.

# How Does It Fit with the Group?

**Strategy** When you come to an unfamiliar word, read the group of words surrounding it and ask yourself, "How do these words fit together? What could I notice that would help me figure out the unfamiliar?"

**What it is** Being explicit about what you mean when you say "use context" can be helpful to children as they work to uncover the meaning of words in their books.

**How I'd teach it** Kevin Cunningham's *Pandemics* (2012) contains the sentence "Infected fleas living on rats also spread plague to rodents throughout the American West. Prairie dogs, squirrels, and many other species remain infected today" (25). To figure out what a *prairie dog* is, readers can group *rodents*, *squirrels*, *rats*, and *species* and ask, "What do these words have in common?" From there, they can deduce that they are all small animals, which suggests that a prairie dog must be some kind of small animal, probably a rodent, like a squirrel.

Further, encourage students to pay attention to words that signal that a word is not a part of the group, such as *not*, *unlike*, *other*, *while*, and *whereas*. When reading Janine Scott's *Glow in the Dark* (2011), students who don't know the meaning of *artificial* can lean on the signal word *other* to figure it out: "Some sources of light, like the sun, are natural. Other sources of light, like lightbulbs, are artificial" (6). Tipped off by the signal word, the reader knows to look for a contrast to *natural* and can deduce that *artificial* means "man-made."

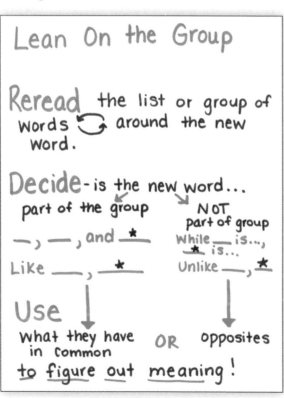

Kelly Boyle

**Who is this for?**

**LEVELS**
M–W

**SKILLS**
monitoring for meaning and using context

# V.13

# Navigate Multiple-Meaning Words

**LEVELS**

M–W

**SKILLS**

monitoring for meaning and using context

**Strategy**  Pause at a word you come upon that has multiple meanings. Reread the sentence closely, thinking about each of the possible meanings. Ask, "Does the meaning I am giving the word make sense here?" If not, try another of the meanings of the word.

**What it is**  Many words have more than one meaning—words such as *light* and *leaves*, *blue* and *bear*—and it's important for students to be able to determine the author's intended meaning of a word to understand the text fully. In *When Kids Can't Read, What Teachers Can Do* (2002), Kylene Beers recommends a great activity called "Words Across Texts." The teacher or student finds words with multiple meanings, such as *pump*. Then students are given questions like "What would the word *pump* mean to a bodybuilder? To a woman who loves shoes? To a gas-station attendant?"

**How I'd teach it**  When reading *Gung Hay Fat Choy* (1982) by June Behrens, readers can apply this strategy when they come to the word *characters*: "There are red and orange scrolls everywhere. The Chinese characters on the scrolls carry messages of Good Health, Luck, Long Life, Prosperity, and Happiness" (16). The reader may infer that *characters* is a word with multiple meanings. The usual definition—people or animals in books or movies—is not the correct one here. If the reader rereads the sentence closely, they may infer that the red and orange scrolls mentioned in the text are banners with Chinese writing. Therefore, this use of *characters* refers to the writing.

Two or More Different Meanings!

1. Pause at a word that has multiple meanings.

2. Reread the sentence closely.

3. Ask, "Does the meaning I'm giving the word make sense here?"

Lauren Knoke

# Go Outside the Text

**Strategy** When you come to a word you don't know, try using your strategies to find the meaning within the text. If you're still not sure, seek out the definition from an outside resource (a dictionary, dictionary.com, etc.). Reread the context in your book with the new definition in mind.

**What it is** At times, the author may assume the reader knows about key words or concepts and won't define them in context or in a glossary. That's when an old-fashioned dictionary or modern-day e-reader comes in handy! One of my favorite things about reading on an e-reader is that you can just scroll and underline any word in any part of the text, and the definition pops up on the bottom of the page. This feature satiates my desire to learn new words and allows me to move quickly to the next sentence knowing I've understood the author's meaning.

**How I'd teach it** Although we may not yet have e-readers for every student, we can give permission for students to get up and consult another source—Google (if you have a computer or tablet in your classroom), a dictionary, or even another text on the same topic. This strategy may be particularly helpful when a child has chosen to read about a topic that is unfamiliar—perhaps one that's interesting but hasn't yet been covered in class, and about which the child has no prior knowledge.

*Who is this for?*

**LEVELS**

M–W

**SKILLS**

monitoring for meaning and using context

Merridy Gnagey

# V.15

# Read Easy-to-Hard

**LEVELS**

M–W

**SKILLS**

monitoring for meaning and using context

**Strategy** Find a collection of books on a topic you want to read about, at a range of text levels (from far easier than what you usually read, to a text that might be a bit of a stretch). Start with the easiest and work your way to the hardest, collecting vocabulary as you go.

**What it is** When a student has chosen to read on a topic they think will be fascinating but that they know little about, it's helpful to teach them to make a plan. Reading easier books on the subject first—even those several levels below what the child typically reads independently—will help them learn vocabulary that is likely to show up in the harder book. You can help facilitate this plan by prebundling books on the same topic or teaching readers how to look in the classroom library.

**How I'd teach it** You might start readers who are interested in reading about gorillas with *Gorilla's Story* (2009) by Harriet Blackford and Manja Stojic, then move on to *What Is a Primate?* (1999) by Bobbie Kalman and H. Levigne, and work up to *Gorillas* (2009) by Seymour Simon. Another way to scaffold students' knowledge is to create multigenre text sets that include biographies. For example, you might include Jeanette Winter's biography *The Watcher: Jane Goodall's Life with the Chimps* (2011) with other books on primates.

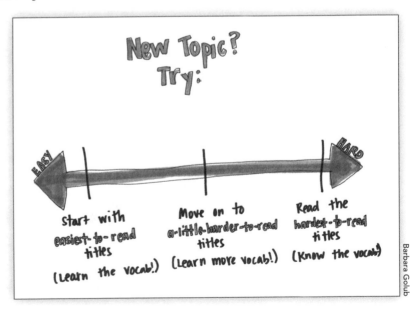

# Create a Word Wall Around a Subject

**Strategy** Collect words that will be important to know about your topic before reading about it. Look in a glossary, peek through the book for bolded words, or talk with friends about what they know about your topic. As you read, add definitions to your personal word wall, and add new words as you find them.

**What it is** Pinpointing words before reading can help focus the reader on key terms to know about a topic. During independent reading, children can create their own "word walls" in a notebook. For class studies, a teacher can pinpoint a few key words and post them in the classroom.

**How I'd teach it** Say you are modeling your nonfiction lessons using books about the Civil Rights Movement. You would probably want readers to know about words such as *boycott*, *segregation*, and *protests*. As your unit progresses, you might add more words to the chart, asking kids to integrate them into their conversations. Students could create their own personalized word walls, using their individual topics to gather expert words.

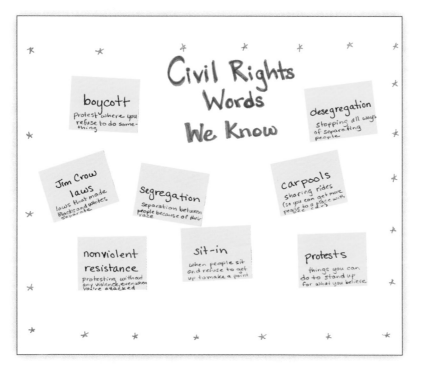

# V.17

# Look Out for Key Words: Cause and Effect

*Who is this for?*

**LEVELS**

M–W

**SKILLS**

monitoring for meaning and using context

**Strategy**   Be on the lookout for words commonly used with cause and effect, such as *if*, *then*, *because*, *so*, *consequently*, *therefore*, *due to*, *since*, *as a result*, *the reason for*, and *thus*. Identify the *cause* in the sentence or paragraph, and the *effect*. Then think, "Given what this part is teaching, what could the word mean?"

**What it is**   Sometimes if readers study a sentence or paragraph's structure, they are able to uncover the meaning of an unfamiliar word. Key words can alert readers to a cause-and-effect relationship.

**How I'd teach it**   Take the sentence from Osborne West's "The Monroe Family" (2002): "When Jim's father died in 1920, his older brother Pearly inherited the land" (86). If the reader is unable to determine the meaning of the word *inherit*, they can first identify the cause and effect within the sentence. Point out that the cause is that the father died and the effect is that Pearly inherited the land. You might say, "Well, if someone dies, they no longer have their possessions, so saying Pearly inherited the land could mean that he was awarded or given the land."

# Literally or Figuratively?

**Strategy**  When the author compares something about the topic you're reading about with something else, ask yourself, "Does the author mean this literally or figuratively?" If figuratively, read around the rest of the text to see what the author could mean by the comparison.

**What it is**  Sometimes nonfiction writers will use figurative language, such as similes or metaphors, to make their writing more engaging, and to bring facts to life. This technique can throw a reader's comprehension for a loop if they read it too literally. Help students look at the larger context of the passage for clues about what point the author is trying to make. Figurative language is an author's craft technique that is common in fiction, poetry, and nonfiction; therefore, students should be encouraged to use this strategy to support their reading of any genre.

**How I'd teach it**  Take the sentence from Martin Jenkins' *Can We Save the Tiger?* (2011): "The companies that make the medicine will lose out on the money they get from selling it and may try to persuade the government not to do anything—who cares about a few ugly vultures, anyway?" (30). Let students consider whether the author literally means that nobody cares about vultures and neither should we. Guide them to think about the whole text and what the author's opinion is about the topic of extinction. They may think together about how in a book about the importance of protecting endangered species, he's being sarcastic to drive home his point.

Who is this for?

**LEVELS**

M–W

**SKILLS**

monitoring for meaning and using context

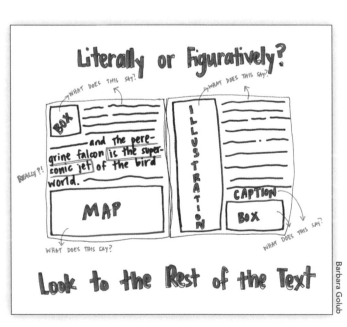

Barbara Golub

# V.19 Quotation Marks as Clues

**Strategy** Pause when you come across a word in quotation marks. Consider whether or not the word is being used figuratively. Think, "What does this word mean in this context?"

**What it is** An author will sometimes help us to determine figurative language by placing quotation marks around words and phrases.

**How I'd teach it** In his article "Hanging by a Thread" (2000), Richard Stone writes, "But Perlman won't be surprised if his 'patient' doesn't make it" (17). Here, *patient* doesn't mean a person or animal Perlman is caring for. Instead, the author is referring to Perlman's fruit seeds. Another example can be found in Marty Crisp's *Everything Dolphin* (2004): "Instead of reading a map, dolphins 'read' the earth's electromagnetic messages" (33). The word *read* is in quotes because although dolphins cannot really read, the signals give them information just as reading gives us information.

Quotation Marks = Clues to Figurative Language

1. Pause when you come across a word in quotation marks.

2. Think, "What does the word mean here?"

Lauren Knoke

# Read the Larger Context

**Strategy** After reading a word's context within a sentence, you may have some idea of what a word means. Next, read a little further, keeping the word and its possible meaning in mind, and ask, "Does what I originally thought still make sense?" If you understand it well enough to explain it, keep reading. If the meaning is still unclear, reread and revise.

**What it is** When the meaning of a word isn't clear, readers need to infer to come up with a probable meaning. This strategy encourages children to keep that inferred meaning in mind and read on to either confirm or revise their thinking.

**How I'd teach it** Take Sarah Irvine's *No Animals, No Plants* (2008). In the section "Why Are Species Endangered?" the word *habitat* appears in the first paragraph— "There are four main reasons why species get into trouble. The most important one right now is habitat destruction"—and again in a photo caption (12–13). Though *habitat* might pose a challenge to some readers, the sentence alone may not offer enough support. It could mean "food" or "home" or "young." Reading on and looking at the surrounding photographs, a reader can likely conclude that it means the place in nature where an animal or plant lives and grows.

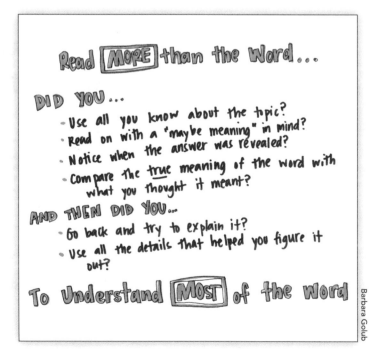

Read [MORE] than the Word...

DID YOU...
- Use all you know about the topic?
- Read on with a "maybe meaning" in mind?
- Notice when the answer was revealed?
- Compare the <u>true</u> meaning of the word with what you thought it meant?

AND THEN DID YOU...
- Go back and try to explain it?
- Use all the details that helped you figure it out?

To Understand [MOST] of the word

Barbara Golub

## Who is this for?

**LEVELS**
O–W

**SKILLS**
monitoring for meaning and using context

# V.21

# Be a Word Surgeon

**LEVELS**

R–W

**SKILLS**

monitoring for meaning and using context

**Strategy** Look for roots, beginnings, and endings of the word(s) you are learning about. Study each part, and use what you know about each part, or where you've seen that same part of a word in another word you know, to make meaning of the whole word.

**What it is** Readers can be like doctors! They can "perform surgery" on words as a way to learn more about them.

**How I'd teach it** Consider using a short text to model with, such as Jan Meyer's "Harry Houdini: Master of Escapes" (2006). You might pause when you come to the sentence "To prepare for his stunt, Houdini had submerged himself in his large bathtub at home and practiced holding his breath for increasingly long periods of time" (8). To dissect the word *submerged*, you might say, "Hmm. The word *submerged* has two parts, *sub* and *merged*. I am thinking about *sub*. Where have I heard this word before? *Submarine* and *subtitle*, just to name two examples. *Submarine* is under the water and *subtitle* is under the title. In both of those words, *sub* means 'under.' *Submerged* must mean 'under something' as well. What was he under? Let's look at the second part of the word together— *merge*. Let's think together, what does *merge* mean?" This sort of think-aloud provides students with a framework that allows them to analyze and understand words as they move into more sophisticated texts.

Marjorie Martinelli

*Vocabulary and comprehension go hand in hand. Our research shows that a higher vocabulary predicts or suggests that a student will comprehend at a higher level. This connection is not just an accident. Really, it is causal. We know that if you work to improve students' vocabulary, it actually improves their comprehension.*

—NELL K. DUKE AND V. S. BENNETT-ARMISTEAD (2003)

Deriving meaning
from a text feature
by synthesizing
information from that
feature, the text, and,
if present, other text
features

# Text Features

For many years, nonfiction reading instruction often centered around teaching the names and functions of text features. They are an important part of the genre! However, if our goal is to teach students how to comprehend deeply, teaching them how to identify text features is not enough. We need to teach them how to understand the information the author is presenting in the feature and how to synthesize that information with information in the rest of the book.

## Deriving Meaning from a Text Feature by Synthesizing Information from That Feature, the Text, and, If Present, Other Text Features

The following strategies help readers unpack information from text features and connect that information to information in the main text. The work readers do from level to level may seem similar, but as levels increase, the amount of text they encounter increases, and the features become more complex. Regardless of the level of book they read, readers need to understand the information an author is communicating in a text feature, and then explain it on its own and in connection with other parts of the text.

Beginning at Level O, text features may give information beyond what the main text has to offer. Therefore, the job of synthesizing the information in the feature with information in the main text becomes more challenging. By the time a reader is navigating books and articles at and around Level Q, text features become more text heavy—almost like sections with their own main ideas and details. At Level U, texts become even denser and more feature filled. Readers must now be able to explain how features relate to one another, as well as to the main text, across a section, a chapter, or even a whole book.

The way a reader "reads" a feature can vary based on the kind of feature it is. In this section, you'll find helpful strategies for teaching children to navigate the following types of features:

- glossaries

- tables of contents

- indexes

- maps

- procedures and activities

- firsthand accounts and profiles of historical figures (often in sidebars)

- reference and resource lists

- illustrations and photographs

- charts and graphs

- timelines

- sidebars

- special text treatments (bold, italics, etc.)

- author notes

# Strategies for Understanding Text Features at a Glance

# Strategies for Understanding Text Features at a Glance

| Strategy | | Levels | Skills | Page |
|---|---|---|---|---|
| TF.15 | Use the Index to Select a Book | O–W | Deriving meaning from a text feature by synthesizing information from that feature, the text, and, if present, other text features | 132 |
| TF.16 | Unpack the Meaning of a Map by Using Map Features | O–W | Deriving meaning from a text feature by synthesizing information from that feature, the text, and, if present, other text features | 133 |
| TF.17 | Make the Most of the Procedure Page | O–W | Deriving meaning from a text feature by synthesizing information from that feature, the text, and, if present, other text features | 134 |
| TF.18 | Learn More from References and Resources | O–W | Deriving meaning from a text feature by synthesizing information from that feature, the text, and, if present, other text features | 135 |
| TF.19 | Shift Perspectives with Firsthand Accounts | P–W | Deriving meaning from a text feature by synthesizing information from that feature, the text, and, if present, other text features | 136 |
| TF.20 | Consider Historical Characters as Fictional Characters | P–W | Deriving meaning from a text feature by synthesizing information from that feature, the text, and, if present, other text features | 137 |
| TF.21 | Read Every Bit of a Chart to Get Every Bit of Information | P–W | Deriving meaning from a text feature by synthesizing information from that feature, the text, and, if present, other text features | 138 |
| TF.22 | Use Your Math When You Come to a Graph | P–W | Deriving meaning from a text feature by synthesizing information from that feature, the text, and, if present, other text features | 139 |
| TF.23 | Don't Skip the Author Notes | P–W | Deriving meaning from a text feature by synthesizing information from that feature, the text, and, if present, other text features | 140 |
| TF.24 | Orient Yourself to a Timeline | R–W | Deriving meaning from a text feature by synthesizing information from that feature, the text, and, if present, other text features | 141 |
| TF.25 | Use a Timeline to Summarize an Understanding | R–W | Deriving meaning from a text feature by synthesizing information from that feature, the text, and, if present, other text features | 142 |
| TF.26 | Organize Your Reading with a Timeline | R–W | Deriving meaning from a text feature by synthesizing information from that feature, the text, and, if present, other text features | 143 |
| TF.27 | Think, "How Can I Use This Sidebar?" | R–W | Deriving meaning from a text feature by synthesizing information from that feature, the text, and, if present, other text features | 144 |

# TF.1

# Use the Glossary as a Warm-Up

## Who is this for?

**LEVELS**

J–W

**SKILLS**

deriving meaning from a text feature by synthesizing information from that feature, the text, and, if present, other text features

**Strategy**  Preview the glossary prior to reading the book to get a sense of the key words and concepts you'll encounter. Identify which words you know well already and which you'll want to learn before you encounter them in the book. Read the definitions for the new words to get a starting definition in your mind before you read.

**What it is**  A glossary contains many terms that are key to understanding a book's topic.

**How I'd teach it**  If you are using *Amazing Animal Facts* (2011) to model this strategy, you might turn to the glossary and think aloud: "Which words do I already know? Let's see. Well, I know the word *army*—it's like a group of soldiers. I've heard of *camouflage*—that's what an animal uses to blend in with the environment. *Migration*—that's when an animal moves from one place to another, usually during a season, I think. Like how birds go south in the winter. Oh, I also know *predator*—that's an animal that hunts and eats another animal. Now, let me see which words I want to know. Hmm. *Amphibian* and *nocturnal* are words I don't know, so I'll read their definitions to warm up my brain before reading the book."

Merridy Gnagey

# Use the Glossary to Review Key Terms

**Strategy** Readers find the glossary when they are done reading. Then they read through the terms to see which words they understand and which terms they are still uncertain about.

**What it is** Readers can check their understanding by reviewing the key terms in a glossary after reading.

**How I'd teach it** If you're using *Amazing Animal Facts* (2011), you might tell students that when they've finished the text, they should check how much they remember by using the glossary as a checklist of sorts. You might say, "I am now going to look at the glossary one more time. This time, after reading the text, I'll scan the list of terms and ask myself, 'Which words do I know now?' Well, I remember *amphibian*, *aquarium*, *army*, and *bird*. Wait, I forgot this word, *burrow*. Let me check the definition of the word. It says 'to dig, or tunnel, underground.' I remember now: that's what certain frogs and toads do during winter."

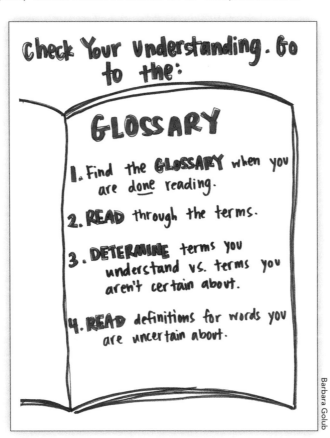

Check Your Understanding. Go to the:

**GLOSSARY**

1. Find the GLOSSARY when you are done reading.

2. READ through the terms.

3. DETERMINE terms you understand vs. terms you aren't certain about.

4. READ definitions for words you are uncertain about.

Barbara Golub

**Who is this for?**

LEVELS

J–W

SKILLS

deriving meaning from a text feature by synthesizing information from that feature, the text, and, if present, other text features

# TF.3

# Use the Glossary to Sound Like an Expert

## Who is this for?

**LEVELS**

J–W

**SKILLS**

deriving meaning from a text feature by synthesizing information from that feature, the text, and, if present, other text features

**Strategy** When you're in the midst of reading about a topic and are getting ready to teach someone else or to write about that topic, you can ask yourself, "Can I use the words of an expert when I am talking about this topic?" Refer to the glossary and revise any vague language with precise language.

**What it is** Part of becoming an expert on a topic is being able to use the language of an expert accurately.

**How I'd teach it** When partners come together to discuss their reading, they could take their books along. One reader might open Sara Swan Miller's *Seahorses, Pipefishes, and Their Kin* (2002) to the glossary and put it on their lap while sharing ideas and work about the book. During the conversation, the reader can remember to use the words of the expert and can glance at the glossary while sharing their understanding of the topic: "Seahorses have body parts to protect them from predators. They have these spikes and bumps called *cirri* all over their bodies."

Use the Glossary to Sound Like an Expert!

Lauren Knoke

# Butterfly In and Out with the Table of Contents

**Strategy**  Read through the table of contents. Ask yourself, "What will be included in this book, based on the chapter titles?" Then ask yourself, "What am I interested in reading first? What questions do I have?" Readers can use the table of contents to jump into a part to answer a question or pursue an interest.

**What it is**  With nonfiction, unlike with fiction, readers can dip in and out of the text, like a butterfly flitting from flower to flower, according to their interests or questions they have about the topic.

**How I'd teach it**  If you are reading Karen Latchana Kenney's *Harsh or Heroic? The Middle Ages* (2008a) and you want to find out about the role of women, you wouldn't have to read the whole book. Instead, you would preview the table of contents and ask, "Which section seems like it is mostly about this topic?" Then you could model how to think aloud: "Hmm. 'Harsh or Heroic?' I am thinking that seems to be mostly about fighting. 'The Order of Things' is likely about different groups of people within society. 'Medieval Women!' That section appears to be mostly about women during medieval times. Bingo! Now, I'll turn to page 24 to answer my question."

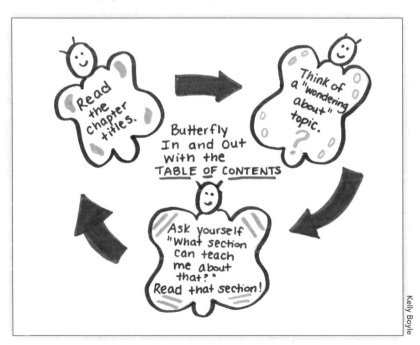

Kelly Boyle

## Who is this for?

**LEVELS**

J–W

**SKILLS**

deriving meaning from a text feature by synthesizing information from that feature, the text, and, if present, other text features

# TF.5

# The Table of Contents: A Key to Text Structure

## Who is this for?

**LEVELS**

J–W

**SKILLS**

deriving meaning from a text feature by synthesizing information from that feature, the text, and, if present, other text features

**Strategy** Approach the table of contents asking, "How is this text structured? How will that help me to determine how I will read this text?"

**What it is** A table of contents acts as a blueprint because it lays out how the text will unfold. Although readers may be accustomed to noticing topics and subtopics in a text, they may be less accustomed to thinking about text organization. Instead of just seeing what topics will be covered in each chapter, readers can approach the table of contents thinking about how topics relate from chapter to chapter. Noticing an overall text structure such as cause and effect, problem/solution, or narrative will help to give the reader a head start on the overall meaning of the book.

**How I'd teach it** If you are modeling this strategy with *Earthquakes* (2003) by Trudi Strain Trueit, you might show readers how you turn to the table of contents and wonder aloud about patterns you see: "I'm noticing that it starts with the actual earthquake, then talks about why earthquakes occur, how to measure them, and the effects of an earthquake. I am thinking that this book is structured in a cause-and-effect format, so I should likely read the sections in order, to truly understand the connection between events."

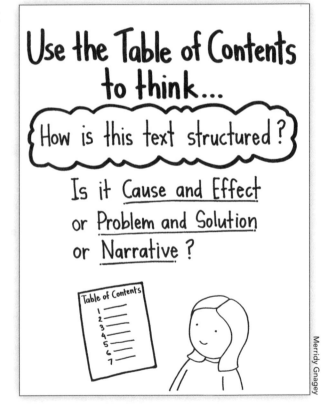

Use the Table of Contents to think...

How is this text structured?

Is it Cause and Effect
or Problem and Solution
or Narrative?

# Understand the Structure of the Index

**Strategy** First, determine key words and phrases. Then ask yourself, "Will this key word appear as a topic or subtopic?" Topics often appear repeatedly throughout a book, but a subtopic may appear in just one or two parts.

**What it is** An index is sometimes broken up into topics and subtopics. Therefore, when using one as a search tool, the reader must be nimble when it comes to looking for key words and phrases.

**How I'd teach it** Take Roland Smith's *Sea Otter Rescue* (1990). If students are interested in learning about ways in which oil spills affect sea animals, they could think about the key phrase *oil spill*. You could wonder aloud: "Would this be a topic or subtopic? Is this something that appears throughout the whole book or just in one part? Well, I am thinking that oil spills are something specific that can happen with oil, so maybe oil is the topic and oil spill might be the subtopic. Now I can scan the index to find those terms."

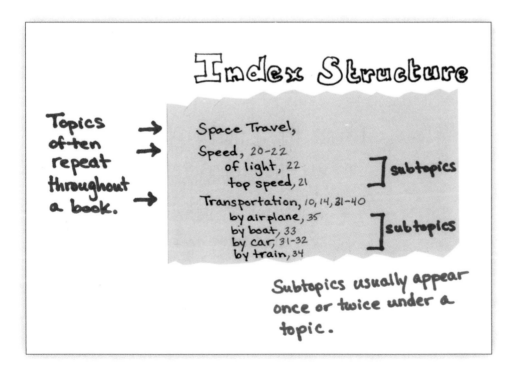

## Who is this for?

**LEVELS**

J–W

**SKILLS**

deriving meaning from a text feature by synthesizing information from that feature, the text, and, if present, other text features

**TF.7**

# Apply Your Knowledge

*Who is this for?*

**LEVELS**

J–W

**SKILLS**

deriving meaning from a text feature by synthesizing information from that feature, the text, and, if present, other text features

**Strategy**  If you find a page in your book with an activity (recipe, experiment, craft), slow down your reading. Read the materials and visualize them in front of you on the table. Pause after each step, imagining yourself doing it. At the end of the procedure, think about what doing the activity (even in your imagination) taught you.

**What it is**  Readers might come to an activity page and either complete the activity or, if they don't have the materials, visualize themselves carrying out the activity step by step.

**How I'd teach it**  Using *Building a Future* (2012a) by Lynette Evans, you might consider modeling how to complete some steps from the activity page at the end of the book and envision doing the rest, to show students two options for how to engage with an activity page: "Step one says, 'Find and name the energy-saving features of the eco-home in this picture.' I am going to pick up my book and point to some of these features. Oh! Here I see solar panels and recycling cans. Then it tells the reader to 'list ways in which your home and habits might harm the environment.' Instead of physically listing them on paper with a pencil, I can list them across my fingers as I make a mental note of each habit."

Apply Your Knowledge!

1. Read the activity page in your nonfiction text.

2. Complete or visualize yourself carrying out the steps.

\* Deeper understanding of the main idea! \*

Lauren Knoke

# Cross-Check Information by Going Outside the Text

**Strategy** Readers of nonfiction examine the resources section with a critical eye. One way we can do this is by studying the resources page and asking, "What resources did this author consult? Are they reliable? Do they help the author to establish credibility on the topic?"

**What it is** The resources section of a nonfiction book, or bibliography, allows the reader to analyze the author's sources critically. Students can look at it and consider the reliability of sources.

**How I'd teach it** Take *Down Down Down* (2009) by Steve Jenkins. At the end of his book, Jenkins includes a list of references to give credit to those people whose information he consulted as he wrote. You could put the list of references of *Down Down Down* under a document camera and wonder aloud about the credibility of some of the sources: "Hmm. The Museum of Natural History is a research museum focusing on animals and people, so they probably know a lot about this topic. I'm thinking that Steve Jenkins did his research there. Therefore, I can likely trust the facts and details provided in his book."

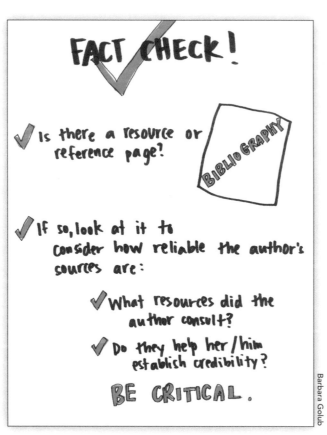

FACT CHECK!

✓ Is there a resource or reference page?

BIBLIOGRAPHY

✓ If so, look at it to consider how reliable the author's sources are:

  ✓ What resources did the author consult?

  ✓ Do they help her/him establish credibility?

BE CRITICAL.

Barbara Golub

## Who is this for?

**LEVELS**

J–W

**SKILLS**

deriving meaning from a text feature by synthesizing information from that feature, the text, and, if present, other text features

# TF.9 Pictures Are Worth a Million Words

## Who is this for?

**LEVELS**

J–W

**SKILLS**

deriving meaning from a text feature by synthesizing information from that feature, the text, and, if present, other text features

**Strategy** First look at a picture as a whole. Then, study it part by part, wondering, "What details do I notice in this picture?" From there, you can read the caption or surrounding text to try to say more about what's in the picture.

**What it is** Because every picture in a nonfiction book is carefully placed on a page, a reader should take the time to analyze them. Pictures sometimes convey more information than what is included in the text, and the author depends on the reader to look at the pictures and learn information.

**How I'd teach it** In Patricia Lauber's *Volcano: The Eruption and Healing of Mount St. Helens* (1986), a photograph shows plants beginning to grow on an overturned tree. Have students examine the photograph and describe what they see. As you model, you might say, "I see plants that are growing on the roots of the tree. Looking closely, it seems like the tree is dead and covered with ash. There is no green coming from the tree itself—these are plants using the soil attached to the roots to grow." Model the difference between really learning information from the photo and just getting the gist, saying something like, "It looks like some plants are growing."

# Zoom In on a Close-Up

**Strategy** Study the large picture first, then analyze the close-up image and ask yourself, "What new information did this picture show me that the other picture didn't?"

**What it is** Sometimes the author provides a detail from a picture—they zoom in on a part of the picture because it illustrates important information the reader needs to know. Readers should understand how to move back and forth from picture to picture.

**How I'd teach it** Consider Marilyn Woolley's *Honeybees at Work* (1998). In a small group, you might model thinking about the close-up by putting the picture on page 8 under a document camera and studying the main image first. Then you could move to the close-up. You might think aloud something like this: "Oh! I think this image is showing us the grubs inside the nursery. In the first image, you are able to see the entire nursery but cannot get a good view of the grubs. The author wants the reader to note that there are tiny larvae inside."

**Who is this for?**

LEVELS

J–W

SKILLS

deriving meaning from a text feature by synthesizing information from that feature, the text, and, if present, other text features

Zoom In on a Close-Up

1. Study the larger picture.

2. Analyze the close-up image.

3. Ask, "What new information did this picture show me that the other picture didn't?"

I learned...

Lauren Knoke

# TF.11

# Watch Out for "Yellow Light" Fonts

## Who is this for?

**LEVELS**

J–W

**SKILLS**

deriving meaning from a text feature by synthesizing information from that feature, the text, and, if present, other text features

**Strategy** Slow down when you see a word has been given special emphasis such as italics, bolding, or underlining. Use your resources and strategies to figure out what the term means before moving on to a new section.

**What it is** Certain font treatments, such as *italics*, **bold**, and underlined words and phrases in nonfiction, are like a yellow light, signaling the reader to slow down and pay attention. They are used to clue the reader in on words and phrases that are important to the text's overall message.

**How I'd teach it** You could use an article like "Powwow Now" from *Scholastic News* (2000) to show readers how often words of great importance are italicized or bolded. Read aloud a sentence in which a word or phrase with special font treatment appears, such as: "Every year, Sequoya and his family go to a big Native American festival or celebration called a **powwow**." Then think aloud: "*Powwow* must be an important word since the author decided to make it bold. A bolded word is one I need to make sure I know. Often, the author gives me help with this, like a glossary or a sidebar showing word meanings. Before reading on, let me search for some more information about this word, *powwow*."

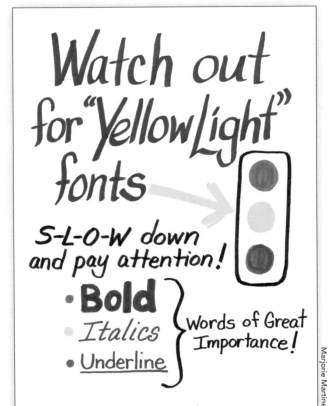

# Visualize the Text by Referring to the Map

 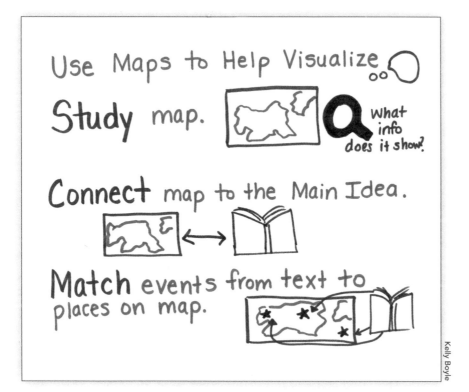

**Strategy** Ask yourself, "What information does the map show me? How does it connect to the main idea(s) on this page?" Then think about (and/or discuss) how you would match the events on the page to the places on the map where those events occur.

**What it is** Sometimes it is tricky for a reader to visualize what's going on in a text, but taking the time to study a visual support, such as a map, can help.

**How I'd teach it** In Patricia Lauber's *Hurricanes: Earth's Mighty Storms* (1996), a map is featured on page 10. You might want to demonstrate how to think aloud with this strategy: "I am thinking that the map is showing the path of the hurricane. The arrow indicates the direction in which it moved. I think this supports the text on the page by highlighting the hurricane's path of destruction and just how many places one storm can affect."

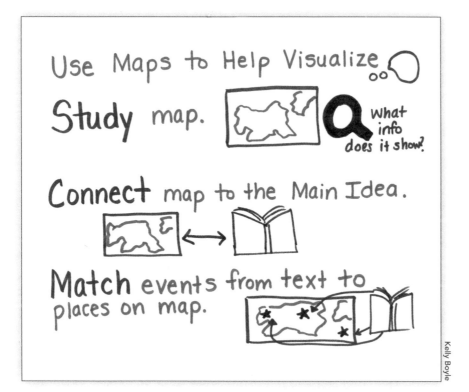

Use Maps to Help Visualize

Study map. what info does it show?

Connect map to the Main Idea.

Match events from text to places on map.

Kelly Boyle

## Who is this for?

**LEVELS**

M–W

**SKILLS**

deriving meaning from a text feature by synthesizing information from that feature, the text, and, if present, other text features

## TF.13 Integrate Multiple Text Features

### Who is this for?

**LEVELS**

O–W

**SKILLS**

deriving meaning from a text feature by synthesizing information from that feature, the text, and, if present, other text features

**Strategy** Look at a group of pictures and captions as a whole rather than each one in isolation, and think, "How do these pictures go together? Does each contribute to a larger point or idea?"

**What it is** The primary purpose of nonfiction texts, especially informational texts, is to share information about science, history, or any topic about the natural or social world (Duke and Bennett-Armistead 2003). Authors select text features such as boxes and images that convey facts and ideas with clarity and immediacy, which compels readers to move forward. When viewed in isolation, text features may not mean much to a young reader, so it is essential to offer lessons that help them see that, together, text features add up to more than the sum of their parts.

**How I'd teach it** Using Penny Arlon's *Planets* (2012), direct students to page 35, where there is a series of images of asteroids, and help them see that by looking at each image in isolation, they can learn a bit about asteroids. However, by looking at them together, the reader can learn the trajectory of an asteroid hitting Earth.

Pairing illustrations with sidebars is another way readers can analyze nonfiction texts. For example, if you are reading Fiona McCormack's article "Creatures of the Deep" (2005), you might wonder aloud why the author paired the table, "Areas and Depths of the Four Major Bodies of Water" with text that discusses how little is known about the world's oceans and how much there is to learn. You could think aloud about how the table provides the reader with statistics on how vast the oceans are. Then you could say, "Oh, maybe that's why humans are constantly learning more and more about the oceans. There is so much to explore."

# Search and Scan with an Index

**Strategy** When researching a topic, you need to first identify the research question, then think about key words and phrases related to that question, and then turn to the index and scan for those words and phrases.

**What it is** An index lists important topics in the text, using key words and phrases. Readers can use them as a tool to locate information within a text that matches their interests and questions.

**How I'd teach it** If a reader is doing a research project on Hurricane Katrina and has Laura Layton Strom's *Built Below Sea Level* (2008a) in their pile of books, that student would first need to remember their research question. If the question is "Why are hurricanes so common in New Orleans?" the student might look for key words such as *hurricanes—locations*, *hurricanes—causes*, or even *hurricanes—maps*. Then the student could quickly turn to the index and search for those words. Upon finding the word *locations*, the student could note the page number indicated in the index, turn to that page, and begin their research.

### Who is this for?

**LEVELS**

O–W

**SKILLS**

deriving meaning from a text feature by synthesizing information from that feature, the text, and, if present, other text features

Barbara Golub

## TF.15 Use the Index to Select a Book

**LEVELS**

O–W

**SKILLS**

deriving meaning from a text feature by synthesizing information from that feature, the text, and, if present, other text features

**Strategy** Use the index as a preview tool. Scan the index and ask yourself, "Do these topics and subtopics sound interesting to me? Is this something I can commit to reading?"

**What it is** There are times when students read one or two pages of a nonfiction book, put it down, and move on to the next title because it was not a good fit for their interests, prior knowledge, or mood. If that happens over and over again, students lose precious reading time—time engaged in reading with stamina.

**How I'd teach it** If you are modeling how to preview Melvin and Gilda Berger's *Howl! A Book About Wolves* (2002b), you might turn to the index and read aloud some of the topics, such as: *alpha wolves*, *habitats*, and *Little Red Riding Hood*. Then you could say, "Wow! I think this book is going to talk about different types of wolves, their homes, and how they are represented in stories. This makes me want to read the book, so I'll add it to my stack." Looking at another book about wolves, a reader might see in the index *wolves and Montana hunting laws*, *Environmental Protection Agencies*, and *sheep farmers*, and consider whether the focus on protection of wolves' habitats is interesting for now.

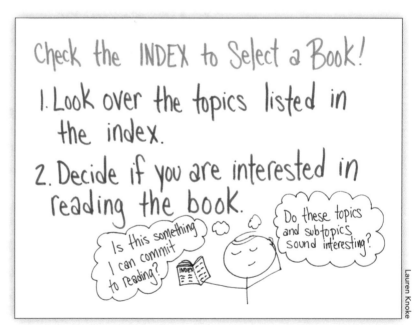

Check the INDEX to Select a Book!
1. Look over the topics listed in the index.
2. Decide if you are interested in reading the book.

Is this something I can commit to reading?

Do these topics and subtopics sound interesting?

Lauren Knoke

# Unpack the Meaning of a Map by Using Map Features

 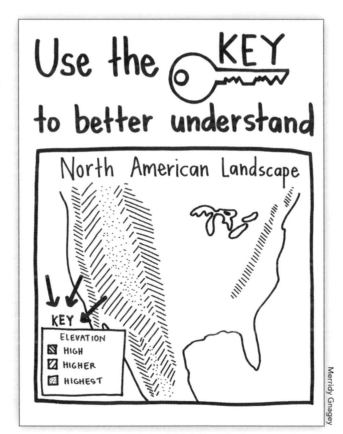

**Strategy** Pause when you come to a map. Look at its features. Study the features to get a better understanding of what the map is teaching you and how it connects to the rest of what you're learning in the section.

**What it is** Maps are peppered with features that help readers navigate them. Titles, color-coded elements, keys, border lines, icons, and arrows are just a few examples.

**How I'd teach it** In Peter Benoit's *Tropical Rain Forests* (2011), a map appears on page 9. You can model how to look for standout features: "I see several features that are important to reading this map. The dark green shading is the first thing that pops out. Let me study those parts closely to better understand this map. Oh, below there is a key that tells the reader that the dark green areas represent tropical rain forests. This tells me that there are rain forests in Central America, South America, Africa, and Asia. Most of them are located in South America."

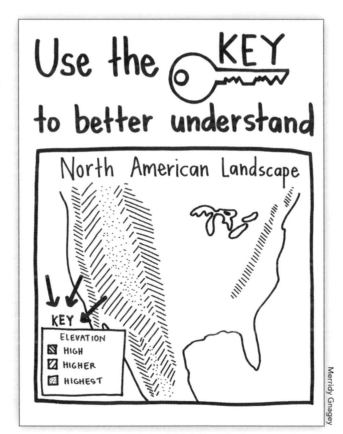

Merridy Gnagey

## Who is this for?

**LEVELS**

O–W

**SKILLS**

deriving meaning from a text feature by synthesizing information from that feature, the text, and, if present, other text features

# TF.17 Make the Most of the Procedure Page

## Who is this for?

**LEVELS**

O–W

**SKILLS**

deriving meaning from a text feature by synthesizing information from that feature, the text, and, if present, other text features

**Strategy**  When you come to a procedure page, read it carefully, visualizing yourself following the steps described. Pause and ask yourself, "What does this do to help explain the topic? How does it connect to the main idea of the text?"

**What it is**  At the end of a nonfiction book, the reader might find a recipe, experiment, or other procedural activity. Nonfiction series such as Scholastic's Investigate books often feature such activities.

**How I'd teach it**  For instance, in Lynette Evans' *Tower Power* (2012b), on pages 24 and 25, a design-a-tower activity is pictured. You might read it aloud for your students, acting out the steps or describing what you're visualizing as you read each step. Then, think aloud: "What does this tower structure do to explain the topic? Well, I am thinking that it might show me how difficult it is to build a sturdy tower. It says, 'They must stand up to nature's howling winds and rattling earthquakes.' How does this connect to the big ideas in the text? I'm thinking that the taller the tower is, the more difficulty it will have remaining upright."

134

# Learn More From References and Resources

**Strategy** When you come to the end of a book that lists references and resources, study those pages and ask yourself, "How could I use this section if I wanted to learn more about what I just read?"

**What it is** The resources section of a nonfiction book, or bibliography, is intended to provide readers with extra information on the subject. Spending time with this section will urge them to seek out further information with questions and ideas in mind, or to add to what they've already learned.

**How I'd teach it** In Trudi Strain Trueit's *Octopuses, Squids, and Cuttlefish* (2002), you might turn to the section "Learning More," which lists websites and other books on these sea creatures, and think aloud: "I could consult these resources if I want to do further research. I could log on to these websites to see what these other sources have to say. Let's see. What I'm most interested in is the octopus. Probably this book by Mary Cerullo and this other one by Andreu Llamas would be good ones to try to find. Oh, and that's a great idea to visit an aquarium and do some of my own observations of live octopuses. I don't live near the Monterey Bay Aquarium, but maybe I'll check out whether the aquarium in New York City has an octopus."

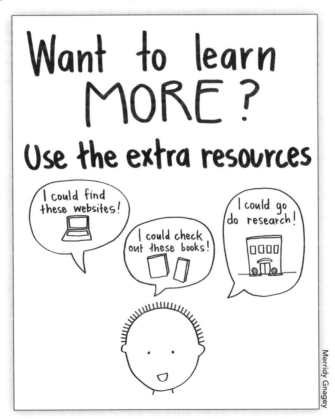

Merridy Gnagey

## TF.19  Shift Perspectives with Firsthand Accounts

### *Who is this for?*

**LEVELS**

P–W

**SKILLS**

deriving meaning from a text feature by synthesizing information from that feature, the text, and, if present, other text features

**Strategy**  Read a firsthand account. Think, "How does this firsthand account provide support to the main idea or ideas in this text?" Reflect, "How does it help me better understand the text?"

**What it is**  In many informational texts, especially those with historical content, firsthand accounts appear—creating a shift from expository to narrative. So the reader must be able to navigate that shift to understand how they work together to support the main idea.

**How I'd teach it**  If you are reading Deborah Kovacs' *Dive to the Deep Ocean: Voyages of Exploration and Discovery* (2000), you might focus on the testimonial of a pilot who worked to recover an H-bomb that was lost at sea near Palomares, Spain: "After hooking a shroud, we would back down the slope, making sure the 'chute was lying flat so we wouldn't get entangled in it. . . . Slowly, we were getting the job done" (20). You might think aloud: "How does this quote connect with the overarching main idea of the section? Well, this section is all about a risky, tense operation that was important for national security and this is the pilot's firsthand story. It helps me understand what it must have felt like to experience the success at the end of the mission."

# Consider Historical Characters as Fictional Characters

**Strategy** Apply what you know about how to understand fictional characters to the real people you read about in your book. Ask yourself, "How does this person's experience shape the way they feel and think?" Then, articulate an idea or conclusion about the kind of person (character traits, theories) the person was.

**What it is** When nonfiction readers encounter a firsthand account of a historical event, they can analyze the historical figure giving the account, as they have learned to do with characters in fiction.

**How I'd teach it** In *Strike! The Farm Workers' Fight for Their Rights* (2014), author Larry Dane Brimner discusses the mistreatment of Filipino farm workers in United States in the mid-1900s. In the beginning of the book, readers learn about the experiences of Larry Itliong, who had successfully negotiated better wages for workers in California who picked grapes. You could voice-over your thinking about how this person's experiences shaped his thinking and feeling: "What caused him to feel this way? Probably being mistreated himself helped him to identify with the other workers. The feelings of injustice helped him to be empowered to help not just himself but also his fellow farm workers. This must have taken tremendous courage given the way that previous strikes ended with violence."

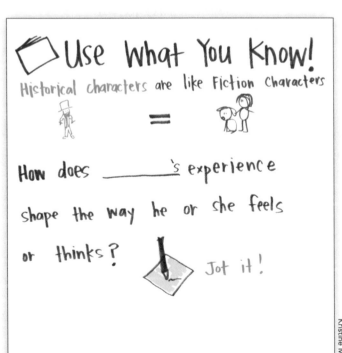

Kristine Mraz

*Who is this for?*

**LEVELS**

P–W

**SKILLS**

deriving meaning from a text feature by synthesizing information from that feature, the text, and, if present, other text features

 **TF.21**

# Read Every Bit of a Chart to Get Every Bit of Information

## Who is this for?

**LEVELS**

P–W

**SKILLS**

deriving meaning from a text feature by synthesizing information from that feature, the text, and, if present, other text features

**Strategy**  Read the chart title first and think, "What will this whole chart be mostly about?" Then, scan information in the chart for details that support the main idea. If there are any callouts or keys to the chart, look at those as well to fully understand what the author is trying to teach.

**What it is**  Charts are sometimes used to summarize important information from the main text; sometimes they are designed to provide extra information. Many readers have a tendency to either zoom right in on charts or breeze past them altogether, when taking a wide-angle view of them might lead to a better understanding of text overall. This strategy encourages readers to linger on charts to learn more.

**How I'd teach it**  Using Lynette Evans' *Animal Armor* (2008), you might model how to read the chart title "Compare Animal Armor," and the subtitles, "Horns," "Antlers," "Tusks," "Spines," and "Bony Plates." Scan to see what each section is telling the reader and then say, "This chart is used to compare and contrast the various body parts animals use to protect themselves."

Kelly Boyle

# Use Your Math When You Come to a Graph

**Strategy** First, read the heading. Then, look to see if there are any keys. Next, read the labels on the axes of the graph. Finally, look to see what story the numbers tell. Try to explain or summarize what you learned from reading the graph.

**What it is** It's important to let readers know that they can call up and apply skills from other curricular areas when they are reading. Teaching them a procedure for getting information from a graph, a skill they may have learned during math, can be helpful during reading.

**How I'd teach it** If you are reading Karen Fanning's article "A Handy Way to Stay Healthy" (2000), have students approach the graph by first studying the title, "Germ Hangouts." Next, they might look for the labels on the axes: "Number of Germs per Square Inch" and "Type of Surface." Then they might notice that the numbers range from 229,000 all the way down to 49 and think, "That's a big range! After looking at the whole thing and all the parts, I can say that this graph is showing the reader the relationship between different surfaces and the number of germs found on each."

Merridy Gnagey

*Who is this for?*

LEVELS

P–W

SKILLS

deriving meaning from a text feature by synthesizing information from that feature, the text, and, if present, other text features

 **TF.23**

# Don't Skip the Author Notes

**Strategy**   Read the author notes/biography. Think, "Who is this author? What authority do they have to write about this topic? Does this author have an agenda? How might their background influence their point of view?"

**What it is**   Author notes can provide readers with critical background information. They often provide information that allows us to analyze the book's ideas a bit more critically, instead of accepting them as unequivocally true. They often provide background on an author that details the author's firsthand experience with the topic, or professional work and recognition in the field, so we can weigh the quality of the information and the author's expertise.

**How I'd teach it**   The author page in *World War II* (1993) reveals how Tom McGowen is specially suited to write about the topic. Have readers note that this author "grew up with an intense interest in military history, and eventually served in the U.S. Navy in World War II." Guide students to understand how his background as a World War II serviceman could have influenced his point of view because he experienced the war firsthand. Discuss how his writing may include an emotional or personal response rather than just the reporting of facts.

Consider Jim Arnosky's *All About Manatees* (2008). You could mull over the information on the author page and think about Arnosky's background. From the author page, we learn he spent years observing manatees in their environments and has written ninety-eight books about wildlife. Wonder aloud: "Does this establish him as an expert on this topic? I think drawing on years of experience with the subject and writing close to 100 books qualifies him as an expert in this area."

# Orient Yourself to a Timeline

**Strategy**  First look at the title. Then scan the dates. Read each event that goes with each date, thinking about how much time passed from event to event. After reading the whole timeline, think about what it has taught you. Relate this information back to what you read in the book so far, thinking, "What new information does this feature provide? Or, does it simply summarize what I've already read?"

**What it is**  Timelines are typically used to outline important events in chronological order. Readers should learn to navigate a timeline and study it to help them remember key moments from the text they read, or to learn new information that wasn't in the main text.

**How I'd teach it**  When demonstrating this procedure, say something like this: "Let's try this with Karen Latchana Kenney's *The Spoils of War* (2008b). The timeline on page 9 is titled 'Milestones of War and Peace.' So I think it is going to summarize important events or maybe even inventions that have to do with war and peace. Next, I see the dates range from 8000 BC to 1945. This timeline covers a great span of time, but I notice there are only seven events listed, so each one must be really important. Now let me look at a few of the points on the timeline. I notice the first point is teaching me about the types of weapons people used from 8000 to 6000 BC. The next event is also about weapons, but a ton of time has passed—about 7,000 years. But here, later in the timeline, it teaches me about rules of war, and then this 1920 to 1946 marker is also about peace. If I were to summarize this whole timeline, I'd say that it has taught me about methods and materials used in war, and also how people try to maintain peace and humane behavior during wartime."

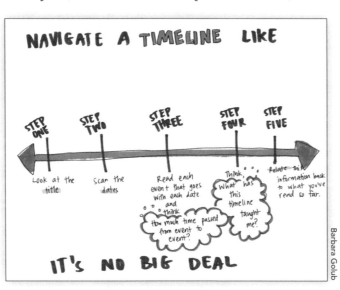

Barbara Golub

**Who is this for?**

**LEVELS**
R–W

**SKILLS**

deriving meaning from a text feature by synthesizing information from that feature, the text, and, if present, other text features

## TF.25 Use a Timeline to Summarize an Understanding

**LEVELS**

R–W

**SKILLS**

deriving
meaning from
a text feature
by synthesizing
information
from that
feature, the text,
and, if present,
other text
features

**Strategy**   Readers can ask themselves, "Can I remember reading about each of the events that are summarized in this timeline?" As you read the event on the timeline, try to elaborate on it using information you read in other parts of the book.

**What it is**   Timelines are a valuable tool to help readers summarize main events. Students can read a listed event on a timeline and use details from the text to support their understanding of that event. Or they can turn to the timeline at the end of a section or the end of a book and use it to check for understanding.

**How I'd introduce this**   This strategy works particularly well with books written on single topics, such as Anne Kamma's *If You Lived When Women Won Their Rights* (2006). This book is about women throughout history fighting for equal rights. Readers can refer to the timeline on page 7 to recap key events in the campaign for women's rights; they can elaborate, using details in the text; and then they can share these details with a partner. With this approach the timeline can serve as an outline for the talk. When a reader elaborates on one event, it might sound something like, "Oh, and then in 1848, the first women's rights convention began in Seneca Falls. They wrote an ad in the newspaper that resembled the Declaration of Independence."

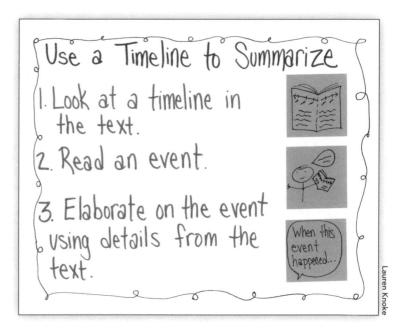

Use a Timeline to Summarize
1. Look at a timeline in the text.
2. Read an event.
3. Elaborate on the event using details from the text.

*Lauren Knoke*

# Organize Your Reading with a Timeline

**Strategy** Scan the timeline first, study its important parts, then begin reading the text. After each section, ask, "Where would this part fit on the timeline?" This allows you to move back and forth between the main text and the timeline.

**What it is** Timelines are a great tool for helping students organize their reading. If students preview the timeline before reading, they can use it to mentally organize details in each section.

**How I'd teach it** Consider Judith Jango-Cohen's *Ellis Island* (2008), which includes a timeline. You could show students how to preview the timeline, scan the dates, and read a bit of the main text, such as, "It is 1907. A small girl stands at the railing of a ship, gripping a ball of yarn in her hands . . . the girl's tears dry in the salty air as her home in Italy disappears." Then you can go back to the timeline to locate the year 1907 and read that almost 900,000 immigrants passed through Ellis Island that year. You might continue with modeling how to move back and forth between the text and the timeline.

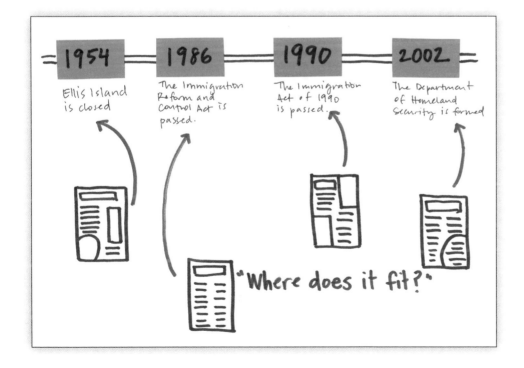

143

# TF.27

# Think, "How Can I Use This Sidebar?"

**Strategy**  When you encounter a sidebar, it may be helpful to first read the main text around the sidebar and then read the sidebar itself, asking, "Does this explain a detail in the text? Or does it give me extra information related to the text?"

**What it is**  Text-filled features like sidebars will become more and more common at higher levels. They sometimes provide extra information to what's in the main text so a reader will need to read them as they do a section (looking for a main idea and details) and then connect what they learn to the main text.

**How I'd teach it**  Take the *Scholastic News* article "Off to Adventure: Lewis and Clark" (2004). Readers can first learn about Lewis and Clark's expedition from the article. Then they can read the sidebar, "Tools for the Trip," and conclude that this connects to a detail in the main text: that Lewis and Clark led a team of almost fifty other explorers. The sidebar helps explain how Lewis and Clark needed to be armed with the proper tools to lead such a large team.

You might also look at *Stormy Weather* (2004) by Julie and Michael Ramsden. Have students read the section titled "Let the Light Show Begin," which is mostly about how lightning occurs and its effects on people, places, and things. When the reader approaches the callout, "Between 1942 and 1947, park ranger Roy Sullivan was struck by lightning seven times!" (9), they are able to determine that this provides a real-life example of just how dangerous lightning can be.

Kelly Boyle

# Bibliography

## Professional Resources

Allington, R. 2001. *What Really Matters for Struggling Readers: Designing Research-Based Programs*. New York: Longman.

———. 2012. *What Really Matters for Struggling Readers: Designing Research-Based Programs*, 3rd ed. New York: Longman.

Baumann, J. F., and E. J. Kame'enui. 1991. "Research on Vocabulary Instruction: Ode to Voltaire." In *Handbook of Research on Teaching the English Language Arts*, edited by J. Flood, J. M. Jensen, D. Lapp, and J. R. Squire, 604–632. New York: Macmillan.

Baumann, J. F., E. J. Kame'enui, and G. Ash. 2003. "Research on Vocabulary Instruction: Voltaire Redux." In *Handbook of Research on Teaching the English Language Arts*, 2nd ed., edited by J. Flood, J. M. Jensen, D. Lapp, and J. Squire. Mahwah, NJ: Lawrence Erlbaum.

Beck, I. L., M. G. McKeown, and L. Kucan. 2013. *Bringing Words to Life: Robust Vocabulary Instruction*, 2nd ed. New York: Guilford Press.

Becker, W. C. 1977. "Teaching Reading and Language to the Disadvantaged—What We Have Learned from Field Research." *Harvard Educational Review* 47: 518–543.

Beers, K. 2002. *When Kids Can't Read, What Teachers Can Do.* Portsmouth, NH: Heinemann.

Betts, E. A. 1946. *Foundations of Reading Instruction, with Emphasis on Differentiated Guidance.* New York: American Book Company.

Calkins, L., and K. Tolan. 2010. *Units of Study for Teaching Reading, Grades 3–5: Navigating Nonfiction.* Portsmouth, NH: Heinemann.

Carver, R. P. 1994. "Percentage of Unknown Vocabulary Words in Text as a Function of the Relative Difficulty of the Text: Implications for Instruction." *Journal of Reading Behavior* 26: 413–437.

Duke, N., and V. S. Bennett-Armistead. 2003. *Reading & Writing Informational Text in the Primary Grades: Research-Based Practices.* New York: Scholastic.

Flippo, R. 2001. *Reading Researchers in Search of Common Ground.* Newark, DE: International Reading Association.

Ford, M. 1992. *Motivating Humans: Goals, Emotions, and Personal Agency Beliefs.* Newbury Park, CA: Sage.

Fountas, Irene C., and Gay Su Pinnell. 2016. F&P Text Level Gradient™. www.fountasandpinnell.com /textlevelgradient/.

Guthrie, J. T., and A. Wigfield, eds. 1997. *Reading Engagement: Motivating Readers Through Integrated Instruction.* Newark, DE: International Reading Association.

Hu, H., and P. Nation. 2000. "Unknown Vocabulary Density and Reading Comprehension." *Reading in a Foreign Language* 13 (1): 403–430.

Krashen, S. 2004. *The Power of Reading: Insights from the Research,* 2nd ed. Santa Barbara, CA: Libraries Unlimited..

Laufer, B. 1988. "What Percentage of Text-Lexis Is Essential for Comprehension?" In *Special Language: From Humans to Thinking Machines,* edited by C. Lauren and M. Nordman, 316–323. Clevedon, UK: Multilingual Matters.

Miller, G. A. 1999. "On Knowing a Word." *Annual Review of Psychology* 50: 1–19.

Nagy, W. E., R. C. Anderson, and P. A. Herman. 1987. "Learning Word Meanings from Context During Normal Reading." *American Educational Research Journal* 24: 237–270.

Nichols, M. 2006. *Comprehension Through Conversation.* Portsmouth, NH: Heinemann.

Petty, G. 2006. *Evidence-Based Teaching: A Practical Approach.* Cheltenham, UK: Nelson Thornes.

Pink, D. 2009. *Drive: The Surprising Truth About What Motivates Us.* New York: Riverhead Books.

Rosenblatt, L. 1978. *The Reader, the Text, the Poem.* Carbondale, IL: Southern Illinois University Press.

Serravallo, J. 2015. *The Reading Strategies Book.* Portsmouth, NH: Heinemann.

———. 2018. *Understanding Texts & Readers.* Portsmouth, NH: Heinemann.

Stanovich, K. E. 1986. "Matthew Effects in Reading: Some Consequences of Individual Differences in the Acquisition of Literacy." *Reading Research Quarterly* 21 (4): 360–407.

Wiggins, G., and J. McTighe. 2001. *Understanding by Design.* Needham Heights, MA: Prentice Hall.

## Children's Literature

Aloian, M., and B. Kalman. 2006. *Endangered Frogs.* New York: Crabtree.

*Amazing Animal Facts.* 2011. New York: Scholastic.

Arlon, P. 2012. *Planets.* New York: Scholastic.

Arlon, P., and T. Gordon-Harris. 2012. *Penguins.* New York: Scholastic.

Arnosky, J. 2008. *All About Manatees.* New York: Scholastic.

Atkinson, M. 2008. *Genius or Madman? Sir Isaac Newton.* New York: Children's Press.

Ballard, R. 1989. *Exploring the Titanic.* New York: Madison Press.

———. 1993. *Finding the Titanic.* New York: Scholastic.

Batten, M. 2000. *Hungry Plants.* New York: Random House.

Behrens, J. 1982. *Gung Hay Fat Choy.* New York: Scholastic.

Benoit, P. 2011. *Tropical Rain Forests.* New York: Children's Press.

———. 2012. *September 11: We Will Never Forget.* New York: Children's Press.

Berger, M. 1999. *Chomp! A Book About Sharks.* New York: Cartwheel Books.

Berger, M., and G. Berger. 2002a. *How Do Frogs Swallow with Their Eyes? Questions and Answers About Amphibians.* New York: Scholastic.

———. 2002b. *Howl! A Book About Wolves.* New York: Scholastic.

———. 2011a. *True or False: Mammals.* New York: Scholastic.

———. 2011b. *Ugly Animals.* New York: Scholastic.

Bishop, N. 2007. *Spiders.* New York: Scholastic.

———. 2009. *Butterflies and Moths.* New York: Scholastic.

Blackford, H., and M. Stojic. 2009. *Gorilla's Story.* London, UK: Boxer Books Ltd.

Brimner, L. D. 2014. *Strike! The Farm Workers' Fight for Their Rights.* Honesdale, PA: Calkins Creek.

"Celebrate Hispanic Heritage." 2007. In *Navigating Nonfiction: Grade 4*, by A. Boynton and W. Blevins. New York: Scholastic.

Coco, P. 2004. "Hip Hoppers." *Scholastic News* 67 (2): 4–5.

Collard, S. 1997. *Animal Dads.* New York: HarperCollins.

"Coming to America." 2003. In *Teaching Students to Read Nonfiction*, by A. Boynton and W. Blevins. New York: Scholastic.

Crisp, M. 2004. *Everything Dolphin.* Chanhassen, MN: NorthWord Books for Young Readers.

Cunningham, K. 2012. *Pandemics.* New York: Scholastic.

Davidson, A. 2008. *A Day in the Life of an African Village.* New York: Children's Press.

Davies, N. 2003. *Surprising Sharks.* Somerville, MA: Candlewick Press.

Davis, K. 2001. *Don't Know Much About the Presidents.* New York: HarperCollins.

Evans, L. 2008. *Animal Armor.* New York: Scholastic.

———. 2012a. *Building a Future.* New York: Scholastic.

———. 2012b. *Tower Power.* New York: Scholastic.

Fanning, K. 2000. "A Handy Way to Stay Healthy." *Scholastic News* 63 (11): 4.

Freedman, R. 1980. *Immigrant Kids.* New York: E. P. Dutton.

Hatkoff, C., I. Hatkoff, and P. Kahumbu. 2006. *Owen & Mzee: The True Story of A Remarkable Friendship.* New York: Scholastic.

Holmes, K. 1998. *Sharks.* Mankato, MN: Bridgestone.

Irvine, S. 2008. *No Animals, No Plants: Species at Risk.* New York: Children's Press.

Jango-Cohen, J. 2008. *Ellis Island*. New York: Scholastic.

Jenkins, M. 2001. *Chameleons Are Cool*. Cambridge, MA: Candlewick Press.

———. 2011. *Can We Save the Tiger?* Cambridge, MA: Candlewick Press.

Jenkins, S. 2009. *Down Down Down: A Journey to the Bottom of the Sea*. Boston, MA: Houghton Mifflin Books for Children.

———. 2010. *Bones: Skeletons and How They Work*. New York: Scholastic.

Jenkins, S., and R. Page. 2001. *Animals in Flight*. New York: Houghton Mifflin.

———. 2003. *What Do You Do with a Tail Like This?* New York: Houghton Mifflin Books for Children.

———. 2010. *How to Clean a Hippopotamus*. Boston, MA: Houghton Mifflin Books for Children.

Kalman, B., and H. Levigne. 1999. *What Is a Primate?* New York: Crabtree.

Kamma, A. 2006. *If You Lived When Women Won Their Rights*. New York: Scholastic.

Kenney, K. L. 2008a. *Harsh or Heroic? The Middle Ages*. New York: Scholastic.

———. 2008b. *The Spoils of War*. New York: Children's Press.

"Kids on the Battlefield." *Scholastic News* 67 (18): 2.

Kinney, J. 2007–2018. Diary of a Wimpy Kid series. New York: Abrams.

Kovacs, D. 2000. *Dive to the Deep Ocean: Voyages of Exploration and Discovery*. Austin, TX: Steck-Vaughn.

Lauber, P. 1986. *Volcano: The Eruption and Healing of Mount St. Helens*. New York: Scholastic.

———. 1996. *Hurricanes: Earth's Mighty Storms*. New York: Scholastic.

Lundell, M. 1999. *Through My Eyes: Ruby Bridges*. New York: Scholastic.

Macdonald, F. 2004. *You Wouldn't Want to Be a Medieval Knight!* New York: Franklin Watts.

Malam, J. 2008. *You Wouldn't Want to Live in Pompeii! A Volcanic Eruption You'd Rather Avoid*. New York: Scholastic.

Markel, M. 2013. *Brave Girl: Clara and the Shirtwaist Makers' Strike of 1909*. New York: Harper Collins.

Marrin, A. 2006. *Oh, Rats!* New York: Dutton Children's Books.

McCormack, F. 2005. "Creatures of the Deep." *Scholastic News* 67 (12): 4–5.

McGovern, A. 2001. *If You Lived in the Days of the Knights*. New York: Scholastic.

McGowen, T. 1993. *World War II*. New York: Children's Press.

Meyer, J. 2006. "Harry Houdini: Master of Escapes." In *25 Nonfiction Passages with Vocabulary Building Crosswords*. New York: Scholastic.

Miller, S. S. 2002. *Seahorses, Pipefishes, and Their Kin*. New York: Franklin Watts.

Newman, S. 2010. *Ancient Greece: A True Book*. New York: Scholastic.

"Off to Adventure: Lewis and Clark." 2004. *Scholastic News* 60 (23): 2.

Patterson, F. 1985. *Koko's Kitten*. New York: Scholastic.

"Powwow Now." 2000. *Scholastic News* 57 (8): 2.

Puleo, C. 2000. "A Lifesaving Hug." *Scholastic News* 62 (18): 6.

Ramsden, J., and M. Ramsden. 2004. *Stormy Weather*. McGraw-Hill X Zone series. Chicago, IL: McGraw-Hill Wright Group.

Rowling, J. K. 1997–2007. Harry Potter series. New York: Scholastic.

Scott, J. 2011. *Glow in the Dark*. New York: Scholastic.

Senior, K. 2010. *You Wouldn't Want to Be a Nurse During the American Civil War!* New York: Franklin Watts.

Simon, S. 2001. *Animals Nobody Loves*. New York: Chronicle Books.

———. 2007. *Snakes*. New York: Scholastic.

———. 2009. *Gorillas*. New York: HarperCollins.

Smith, R. 1990. *Sea Otter Rescue: The Aftermath of an Oil Spill*. New York: Scholastic.

Snicket, L. 1999–2006. Series of Unfortunate Events series. New York: Harper Collins.

Solheim, J. 1998. *It's Disgusting and We Ate It! True Food Facts from Around the World and Throughout History*. New York: Aladdin.

Stanborough, R. 2016. *The Golden Gate Bridge*. Mankato, MN: Capstone.

Stone, L. M. 1984. *Endangered Animals*. Chicago, IL: Children's Press.

Stone, R. 2000. "Hanging by a Thread." *Discover Magazine* Feb. 1, 2000.

Strom, L. L. 2007. *The Egyptian Science Gazette: Where the News Is Ancient History*. New York: Children's Press.

———. 2008a. *Built Below Sea Level: New Orleans*. New York: Children's Press.

———. 2008b. *Caught with a Catch: Poaching in Africa*. New York: Scholastic.

Taylor, L. R. 2000. *Sharks and Other Sea Creatures*. Pleasantville, NY: Reader's Digest Children's Books.

"Thanksgiving: Myth and Fact." 2001. *Scholastic News* 58 (3): B1.

Trueit, T. S. 2002. *Octopuses, Squids, and Cuttlefish*. New York: Watts Library.

———. 2003. *Earthquakes*. New York: Watts Library.

Venezia, M. 1995. *Wolfgang Amadeus Mozart*. Chicago, IL: Children's Press.

Weatherford, C. 2005. *A Negro League Scrapbook*. New York: Scholastic.

West, O. 2002. "The Monroe Family." In *Teaching Students to Read Nonfiction*, by A. Boynton and W. Blevins. New York: Scholastic.

Winter, J. 2011. *The Watcher: Jane Goodall's Life with the Chimps*. New York: Schwartz and Wade.

Woolley, M. 1998. *Honeybees at Work*. Mahwah, NJ: Troll Communications.